On Power
and Ideology

On Power and Ideology

THE MANAGUA LECTURES

Noam Chomsky

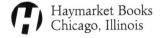

Haymarket Books
Chicago, Illinois

This edition published in 2015 by
Haymarket Books
P.O. Box 180165
Chicago, IL 60618
773-583-7884
www.haymarketbooks.org
info@haymarketbooks.org

ISBN: 978-1-60846-400-5

Trade distribution:
In the US, Consortium Book Sales and Distribution, www.cbsd.com
All other countries, Publishers Group Worldwide, www.pgw.com

This book was published with the generous support of Lannan Foundation
and Wallace Action Fund.

Cover design by Josh On. Cover photo of *Pravda*'s printing presses in 1982 by
Vladimir Rodionov.

Library of Congress Cataloging-in-Publication Data is available.

Entered into digital printing May, 2022.

Table of Contents

Preface to the 2015 Edition

The chapters that follow are based on lectures given in Managua in 1986, at the peak of Reagan's terrorist war against Nicaragua. The lectures took place at about the time when the International Court of Justice condemned the United States for "the unlawful use of force"—aka international terrorism—and ordered it to cease the crimes and pay substantial reparations. The court was haughtily dismissed as a "hostile forum" by the editors of the *New York Times*, offended that it should dare condemn the United States for its crimes. For some years, the United States was joined in defiance of the World Court by Muammar Qaddafi and Enver Hoxha, but Libya and Albania have since complied with the Court judgments, leaving the United States in the splendid isolation it proudly occupies on many international issues.

The essential problem that the United States faces in the world was explained by State Department legal advisor Abram Sofaer. The world majority, he observed, "often opposes the United States on important international questions," so that we must "reserve to ourselves the power to determine" which matters fall "essentially within the domestic jurisdiction of the United States, as determined by the United States," in this case, international terrorism that was intended to punish and devastate the country where I was lecturing—or in approved Orwellian translation, to bring it the blessings of freedom and democracy.

At the same time the cultural correspondent of the *New York Times*, Richard Bernstein, explained in the *Times Magazine* the world was out of step because of various psychological and social maladies. His article was accordingly entitled "The U.N. versus the U.S.," not "the U.S. versus the U.N."

The pathologies of the world continue. In December 2013, the BBC reported the results of an international Gallup poll showing that the United States was regarded as the greatest threat to world peace by an overwhelming margin. No one else even came close. Fortunately, the Free Press spared the American public this further evidence of global backwardness.

At the time of these lectures, in March 1986, Reagan's terrorist war was taking its toll in many ways. A minor one was regular power failures, so that the talks were constantly interrupted until the sound system could come back on. That of course was the least of it. The goal of the terrorist attack, as privately conceded by Administration officials, was to "debilitate the Sandinistas by forcing them to divert scarce resources toward the war and away from social programs" (45), a fact that aroused little comment in the civilized West.

That policy made good sense. It was directed rationally to the threat posed by Nicaragua, "the threat of a good example," to borrow the title of a study by the development agency Oxfam, which reported that Nicaragua was "exceptional" among the seventy-six countries where Oxfam worked in the government's commitment "to improving the condition of the people and encouraging their active participation in the development process." Oxfam's judgments were confirmed by the World Bank and the Inter-American Development Bank. Another sign of Sandinista criminality was that they accepted Costa Rican–initiated diplomatic efforts that the United States was desperately seeking to evade while claiming that they were being blocked by Nicaragua. Perhaps the ultimate crime was to conduct free elections in 1984

that were carefully monitored and judged free and fair, despite
massive U.S. efforts to disrupt them (83f.)—elections that took
place only in the world, but not within the rigid U.S. doctrinal
system that prevails to this day.

In the terminology of U.S. planners, the threat of a good example is rephrased as the threat that one rotten apple can spoil
the barrel, that a virus can spread contagion, that the dominoes
may fall. Another version, explicit in internal documents, is that
successful independent development in a poor country subjected
to U.S. control might inspire others facing similar problems to
pursue the same course, so that the whole system of imperial
domination will erode. As discussed below, this is a leading
theme of Cold War history, masked in fanciful tales of defense
against enemies of awesome power, like Nicaragua. At the time
of these lectures, President Reagan declared a national emergency because of the dire threat to U.S. national security posed
by the government of Nicaragua, which had armies poised only
two days' marching time from Harlingen, Texas. But in his best
John Wayne pose, Our Leader was prepared to confront the ter-
rifying enemy about to overwhelm us.

The driving fears were expressed eloquently by President
Lyndon Johnson, an authentic man of the people, addressing
U.S. troops in Asia. LBJ plaintively told the soldiers that they
were protecting us from the billions of people of the world, who
vastly outnumber us, and if they could would sweep over us and
take what we have (41). So we'd better stop them in Vietnam
while we still have a chance to survive.

Such fears have deep roots in American culture. They appear
in the Declaration of Independence, where Jefferson lamented
the fate of the innocent colonists subjected to the vicious policies
of King George of England, who "excited domestic insurrections
amongst us, and has endeavoured to bring on the inhabitants of
our frontiers, the merciless Indian Savages, whose known rule of

warfare is an undistinguished destruction of all ages, sexes and conditions," words intoned solemnly every July 4. There followed fears of all sorts of other awesome and demonic enemies. Small wonder that to this day courageous souls carry guns on their hips when they venture to the corner store for a cup of coffee.

Inflamed and pathetic rhetoric aside, the actual threats of good examples abroad—not to speak of resistance by the oppressed at home—have been real, and go a long way toward explaining U.S. policies in the world since World War II, with ample precedents in earlier imperial systems, or, for that matter, within the smaller domains of the former junior superpower.

In the first two lectures I attempted to outline, as best I could, what seem to me to be the primary guiding principles of policy decisions: "the commitment of the state to serving private power in the domestic and international arena and the commitment of the ideological institutions to limiting popular understanding of social reality," policies that "are firmly rooted in the institutional structure of the society and are highly resistant to change" (126). Lecture three seeks to apply the doctrines of global management to Central America. The two final lectures turn to the United States itself, to national security policy during the post–World War II era and to the domestic scene, in particular, to the "very limited form of democracy" that exists under capitalist democracy.

The conclusions of the first two lectures are, I think, well confirmed by events since. Particularly informative is the impact of the collapse of the Soviet Union, which eliminated the primary pretext for the policies of the preceding years: defense of all civilized values from the machinations of the Kremlin "slave state," whose "fundamental design" and "implacable purpose" was to gain "absolute authority over the rest of the world," destroying "the structure of society" everywhere—in the terminology of NSC 68 of 1950, one of the most influential internal documents in setting policy for the postwar era. A few years after these lectures, the Cold War ended with the collapse of the global enemy. For those who want to understand the Cold War era, an obvious question is: what happened when the slave state disintegrated?

The answer is straightforward: little changed, except that earlier policies were pursued more intensively. Consider NATO. According to doctrine, NATO was established to protect Western Europe (and the world) from the Russian hordes. What happened, then, when the Russian hordes disappeared? Answer: NATO expanded to the East, in violation of verbal agreements with Mikhail Gorbachev, reaching right to the borders of Russia in ways that are by now raising a serious threat of confrontation. The official role of NATO was also changed. Its mandate became control over the global energy system, sea lanes, and pipelines, while it serves in effect as a U.S.-run intervention force.

Shortly after the Berlin Wall fell, the United States invaded Panama in order to kidnap a minor thug, Manuel Noriega, who had fallen out of favor when he began defying U.S. orders. U.S. forces bombed poor residential areas, killing many people, several thousand according to Central American human rights organizations. After a vulgar assault on the Vatican Embassy where Noriega had taken refuge, U.S. forces apprehended him and brought him to the United States where he was tried and sentenced mostly for crimes that Washington had praised when he was committing them while on the CIA payroll. The shameful episode was not particularly novel, apart from the pretext: no more Russians, so we were defending ourselves from Hispanic narcotraffickers. Other pretexts were developed later as circumstances required.

With the slave state gone, the Bush I administration issued a new National Security Strategy and military budget. The basic message was that things would remain much the same, but with new pretexts. A huge military establishment was still necessary because of the "technological sophistication" of Third World powers. It was necessary to maintain "the defense industrial base," in part a euphemism for high-tech industry that is substantially subsidized through the Pentagon system in our free-market economy. We must continue to maintain intervention forces targeting the crucial Middle East region, where the serious threats we had faced "could not have been laid at the Kremlin's door," contrary to decades of pretense, now abandoned, with the recognition that the primary threat had always been "radical nationalism."

Nuclear weapons strategy also had to be reconsidered. The leading problem was to determine "The Essentials of Post-Cold War Deterrence"—the title of a partially declassified study issued in 1995 by President Clinton's Strategic Command (STRATCOM), which is in charge of nuclear weapons. The study concludes that after the Soviet collapse, nuclear weapons "seem destined to be the centerpiece of U.S. strategic deterrence for the foreseeable future." We must retain the right of "first use" of nuclear weapons, even against non-nuclear states, and make it clear that our actions may "either be response or preemptive." Nuclear weapons must always be readily available because they "cast a shadow over any crisis or conflict," with the obvious implications. We should also not "portray ourselves as too fully rational and cool-headed. . . . That the US may become irrational and vindictive if its vital interests are attacked should be a part of the national persona we project." For our strategic posture, it is "beneficial" if some parts of the decision-making apparatus "may appear to be potentially 'out of control,'" thus posing a constant threat of nuclear attack—a resurrection of the "madman theory" attributed to Richard Nixon.

The Clinton Administration went on to present its geostrategic doctrine, which asserts that the United States is free to resort to "unilateral use of military power," if deemed necessary, to ensure "uninhibited access to key markets, energy supplies and strategic resources." A less expansive version, the Bush II doctrine of preemptive war, was implemented a few years later with the U.S.-UK invasion of Iraq, the worst international crime of the new millennium, with consequences that are now tearing not just Iraq but the whole region to shreds.

More was learned about the extreme dangers of nuclear weapons even when their use is not contemplated, including the years just prior to these lectures. A November 2014 study of the years 1977 to 1983 in the *Bulletin of Atomic Scientists* estimated "false alarms that could be perceived as nuclear attacks" in the range of 43 to 255 per year, and speculated that not much may have changed since. The study concludes that "nuclear war is the black swan we can never see, except in that brief moment when it is killing us. We delay eliminating the risk at our own peril. Now is the time to address the threat, because now we are still alive."

During the years of these threatening false alarms, the Reagan Administration launched operations to probe Russian air and naval defenses, simulating attacks and even a full-scale release of nuclear weapons, along with a high-level nuclear alert intended for the Russians to detect. These actions were undertaken at a very tense moment. Pershing II strategic missiles were being deployed in Europe, with a five- to ten-minute flight time to Moscow, and Reagan announced the SDI (Star Wars) program, which is understood on all sides to be effectively a first-strike strategy. That led to a major war scare in 1983. Newly released archives reveal that the danger was even more severe than had been previously assumed by analysts. A very detailed recent study based on extensive U.S. and Russian intelligence records concludes that "the War Scare Was for Real," and that U.S. intelligence may have underestimated Russian concerns and the threat of a Russian preventive nuclear strike.

In September 2013, the BBC reported that during this dangerous period, Russia's early-warning systems detected an incoming missile strike from the United States, sending the highest-level alert. The protocol for the Soviet military was to retaliate with a nuclear attack of its own. The officer on duty, Stanislav Petrov, decided to disobey orders and not report the warnings to his superiors. Thanks to his dereliction of duty, we are alive to reflect on the black swan we prefer not to see. Other studies reveal a shocking array of close calls, even apart from the "most dangerous moment in history" during the Cuban missile crisis of 1962.

An enormous gap in these lectures, not appreciated at the time, was that another and even more ominous threat was inexorably advancing: environmental catastrophe. By now no reasonable person can doubt that we are marching resolutely toward a grim fate, and not far in the future, unless the course we are following is radically altered.

Meanwhile, the neoliberal assault on the population that gained force under Reagan has taken an increasing toll, particularly after the collapse of the housing bubble in 2008 and the ensuing financial meltdown, the worst blow to the international economy since the Great Depression.

The accompanying decline of functioning democracy proceeds on course. Recent studies in academic political science reveal that a considerable majority of the population, at the lower end of the income scale, are effectively disenfranchised: their preferences have no detectable effect on policy. Influence slowly increases along with wealth until the very top, a fraction of one percent, where policy is largely determined. Formal democracy remains, but in a system perhaps more accurately termed "plutocracy."

It seems that much of the population is reasonably well aware of these tendencies, which proceed in parallel with dramatically rising economic inequality. In a careful study of the November 2014 elections, political scientists Walter Dean Burnham and

Thomas Ferguson show that the decline in voting is reaching the levels of the early nineteenth century, when voting was limited to propertied white males. "Many are convinced that a few big interests control policy [and] crave effective action to reverse long-term economic decline and runaway economic inequality," they write, though no changes "on the scale required will be offered to them by either of America's money-driven major parties."

The lectures end with the observation that institutions are not fixed, that history is not at an end, and that the future offers "many severe threats and many hopeful possibilities."

That remains both true and critically important. Not just for contemplation, but as a stimulus for action.

Preface

In the first week of March, 1986, I had the opportunity to visit Managua and to lecture at the Universidad Centroamericana (UCA), at the invitation of Rector César Jerez, S.J., and also under the auspices of the research center of CIDCA, directed by Galio Gurdián. These lectures consisted of a morning series devoted to problems of language and knowledge, and a late afternoon series devoted to contemporary political issues. Participants included a wide range of people from the academic community and many others in Nicaragua, as well as visitors from Costa Rican universities and foreigners visiting or working in Nicaragua. The lectures, which I delivered in English, were expertly translated into Spanish for the listening audience by Danilo Salamanca and María-Esther Zamora, who translated the public discussion as well. The proceedings were broadcast (and, I subsequently learned, picked up by short wave in the United States) and transcribed, including the discussions afterward, though inevitably many of the thoughtful and informative comments from the floor were not captured properly on the tape recorder and hence do not appear here.

The chapters that follow consist of somewhat extended versions of the afternoon lectures on contemporary political issues and an edited version of the transcripts of the discussion. The morning lectures and discussion will appear in a separate volume, to be published by MIT Press in Cambridge, with the title *Language and Problems of Knowledge*. In attempting to reconstruct the discussion from the transcript, I added material that was missing from the tape in a few places and I have sometimes transferred the discussion from one place to another where it fits more naturally with the edited lectures. Particularly in the transcripts of the afternoon discussion, I have also eliminated a considerable amount of material that I was able to incorporate into the text of the lectures, essentially in response to queries and interventions by the audience. These interventions appear only in fragmentary form below, in part because of this editing, in part because of the technical difficulty of recording speakers from the large and diffuse audience in a bilingual discussion, which proceeded with remarkable facility thanks to the translators and good will of the participants. The published transcripts therefore give only a very limited indication of the stimulating nature of the comments and questions during the lively and open discussion periods, which were all too short because of the constraints of time.

I would like to express particular thanks to Danilo Salamanca and María-Esther Zamora, not only for the careful way in which they carried out the difficult and trying task of translation in both directions, but also for their assistance to me in preparing the lectures. I was particularly pleased that Claribel Alegría agreed to undertake the translation of both volumes into Spanish—both my English text and the discussion transcripts—for the Nicaraguan edition. The English version that appears here, prepared for publication a few months later, includes supplementary documentation and further editing, along with some bibliographical notes at the end.

I would also like to express my thanks—here speaking as well for my wife, Carol, who accompanied me on this visit—to César Jerez, Galio Gurdián, Danilo Salamanca and María-Esther

Zamora, Claribel Alegría, and the many others who spent so much time and effort in making our visit a most memorable occasion for us. We much appreciate the gracious hospitality and care of the many friends, from many walks of life, whom we met in Managua, and the opportunity for very informative discussions with them, and even for some travel and informal visits at their homes, interspersed in a demanding but exhilarating schedule of meetings and lectures. I would also like to thank many people whose names I do not know or remember: the sisters of the Asunción order who welcomed us in the agricultural cooperative they organized in an impoverished peasant community near León, the participants in the public meetings and other discussions, and many others. I might mention particularly the opportunity to meet many people from the wonderful community of exiles from the U.S.-installed horror chambers in the region, who have fled to a place where they can be free from state terror and can live with some dignity and hope—though the Master of the Hemisphere is doing what it can to prevent this grave threat to "order" and "stability."

I expected that Nicaragua would be very different from the picture that filters through the U.S. media, but I was pleased to discover how large the discrepancy is, an experience shared with many other visitors, including people who have lived for extended periods in many parts of the country. It is quite impossible for any honest visitor from the United States to speak about this matter without pain and deep regret, without shame over our inability to bring other U.S. citizens to comprehend the meaning and the truth of Simón Bolívar's statement, over 150 years ago, that "the United States seems destined to plague and torment the continent in the name of freedom"; and over our inability to bring an end to the torture of Nicaragua, and not Nicaragua alone, which our country has taken as its historical vocation for over a century, and pursues with renewed dedication today.

LECTURE 1

The Overall Framework of Order

In these lectures, I will be concerned with United States policy in Central America in the contemporary period. But I want to consider this question in a much broader context. What the United States is doing today in Central America is not at all new, and it is not specific to Latin America. We mislead ourselves by viewing these matters in too narrow a focus, as is commonly done in journalism and much of scholarship, both in the United States and elsewhere.

Surveying the historical record, we do find some variation in U.S. policies. The continuities, however, are much more striking than the variation, which reflects tactical judgments and estimates of feasibility. The persistent and largely invariant features of U.S. foreign policy are deeply rooted in U.S. institutions, in the distribution of power in the domestic society of the United States. These factors determine a restricted framework of policy formation that admits few departures.

Planning and action are based on principles and geopolitical analyses that are often spelled out rather clearly in internal documents. They are also revealed with much clarity by the historical record. If these principles are understood, then we can

1

comprehend quite well what the United States is doing in the world. We can also understand a good deal of contemporary history, given the power and influence of the United States. Current U.S. policies in Central America also fall into place, fitting historical patterns that change very little because of the relatively constant nexus of interests and power from which they arise.

I would like to address these questions in a fairly general way in my first two lectures, turning specifically to Central America in the third. In the fourth lecture, I want to shift the focus of discussion to U.S. national security policy and the arms race, to factors in the international arena that may well terminate history before the immediate problems that concern us can be effectively addressed. In the final lecture, I will turn to domestic U.S. society and ask how foreign policy and national security policies are fashioned. I will also want to inquire into the possibilities for modifying them, a profoundly important matter. The fate of Central America, and in fact the continued existence of human society on this planet, depend to no small extent on the answers to these questions.

Let us turn now to a review of some of the systematic patterns of U.S. foreign policy, beginning with a few general principles that I will then illustrate with various specific examples.

The first principle is that U.S. foreign policy is designed to create and maintain an international order in which U.S.-based business can prosper, a world of "open societies," meaning societies that are open to profitable investment, to expansion of export markets and transfer of capital, and to exploitation of material and human resources on the part of U.S. corporations and their local affiliates. "Open societies," in the true meaning of the term, are societies that are open to U.S. economic penetration and political control.

Preferably, these "open societies" should have parliamentary democratic forms, but this is a distinctly secondary consideration.

Parliamentary forms, as we shall see, are tolerable only as long as economic, social and ideological institutions, and the coercive forces of the state, are firmly in the hands of groups that can be trusted to act in general accord with the needs of those who own and manage U.S. society. If this condition is satisfied, then parliamentary forms in some client states are a useful device, ensuring the dominance of minority elements favored by U.S. elites while enabling the U.S. political leadership to mobilize its own population in support of foreign adventures masked in idealistic rhetoric ("defense of democracy") but undertaken for quite different purposes. In its actual usage, the term "democracy," in U.S. rhetoric, refers to a system of governance in which elite elements based in the business community control the state by virtue of their dominance of the private society, while the population observes quietly. So understood, democracy is a system of elite decision and public ratification, as in the United States itself. Correspondingly, popular involvement in the formation of public policy is considered a serious threat. It is not a step towards democracy; rather, it constitutes a "crisis of democracy" that must be overcome. The problem arises both in the United States and in its dependencies, and has been addressed by measures ranging from public relations campaigns to death squads, depending on which population is targeted. We will turn to examples as we proceed.

What all of this means for much of the Third World, to put it crudely but accurately, is that the primary concern of U.S. foreign policy is to guarantee the freedom to rob and to exploit.

Elsewhere, I have referred to this as "the Fifth Freedom," one that was not enunciated by President Franklin Delano Roosevelt when he formulated the famous Four Freedoms, which were presented as the war aims of the Western allies during World War II: Freedom of Speech, Freedom of Worship, Freedom from Want, and Freedom from Fear. The history of Central America and the Caribbean—and not these regions alone—reveals just how these

fine words are to be understood: as a means to gain public support for crusades in defense of the Fifth Freedom, the one that
really counts.

In the perception of U.S. planners, which is not inaccurate,
the world is peopled with enemies of the Fifth Freedom, who
seek to impede the free exercise of our fundamental right to rob
and to exploit. Among the most dangerous and threatening,
throughout U.S. history, we find Britain, France, Germany, Japan
and other industrial powers belonging to what is now called "the
First World." U.S. expansion and intervention in the Western
Hemisphere has been guided by concern over various of these
enemies since its origins, and the same was true of the conquest
of the Philippines at the turn of the century, which left several
hundred thousand Filipinos dead and much of the U.S. military
command facing court martial for brutal atrocities (for which they
received trifling sentences), an operation undertaken to ensure
that the United States would have a favored position in the competition to control the wealth and markets of Asia. President
Woodrow Wilson's famous rhetorical flourishes during World War
I concealed measures by which the U.S. displaced Britain from
Central America, taking over control of Guatemalan petroleum
resources, for example. During World War II, the U.S. exploited
Britain's travail to expand its influence and control at Britain's expense in Latin America, Asia and the Middle East.

The U.S. has consistently been "anti-imperialist," in the
sense that it has opposed and sought to dismantle the imperial
preference systems established by Britain and lesser powers. The
meaning of this "anti-imperialism" is hardly obscure to its Third
World victims, or to competing imperial powers displaced by
these operations.

As conflicts over this matter erupted within the Western alliance during World War II, the British Colonial Office observed
that "the Americans are quite ready to make their dependencies

politically 'independent' while economically bound to them and see no inconsistency in this" as "American imperialism" is attempting "to elbow us out" in many parts of the world, relying on its overwhelming economic and military power facilitated with trusteeship schemes and other devices to ensure U.S. control. Such measures were legitimate, U.S. planners explained: even though other imperial systems were being dismantled, "these reservations" in favor of the United States "were being made in the interest of world security rather than of our own security . . . what was good for us was good for the world," so Abe Fortas explained, in internal U.S. government discussion. Needless to say, such idealistic thoughts scarcely impressed Europeans who were being displaced by the expanding U.S. neo-colonial system, for example, Winston Churchill, who "viewed American trustees hip schemes as mainly a cover for annexationist plans" (Wm. Roger Louis notes in the major scholarly study of these operations, referring here to the Pacific region). In the crucial Middle East region as well, U.S. interests displaced British and French competitors during and after the war by a combination of economic measures and legal chicanery, based ultimately on the realities of power.

As for Latin America, U.S. ideas were clarified in May 1945 by Secretary of War Henry Stimson, well-known to Nicaraguans for his role in the Marine invasion of the late 1920s that established the rule of the National Guard and the Somoza dictatorship. In private discussion on the need to eliminate all regional systems dominated by other powers, in particular the British, while maintaining and extending our own regional system in Latin America, Stimson explained: "I think that it's not asking too much to have our little region over here [namely, Latin America] which never has bothered anybody."

Similarly, in 1973, in his "Year of Europe" address, Henry Kissinger warned that the Atlantic alliance was endangered because Europe might develop a trading bloc including North

Africa and the Middle East that would raise barriers to U.S. access, failing to comprehend that the role of the European states is to pursue their "regional interests" within an "overall framework of order" managed by the United States. The United States may have "little regions" here and there that it dominates, but not its competitors. More generally, the United States favors "open access" for everyone, as long as its own economic power is so overwhelming (with latent military force at hand if things go wrong) that U.S. corporations are well-placed to win the competition. On the same reasoning, Britain firmly supported "free trade" during the period of its hegemony.

The U.S. conception of "open access" is marvelously expressed in a State Department memorandum of April 1944 called "Petroleum Policy of the United States," dealing with the primary resource. There must be equal access for U.S. companies everywhere, the memorandum explained, but no equal access for others. The U.S.-dominated Western Hemisphere production (North America was the leading oil exporter until 1968), and this dominant position must be maintained while U.S. holdings expand elsewhere. U.S. policy, the document asserted, "would involve the preservation of the absolute position presently obtaining, and therefore vigilant protection of existing concessions in United States hands coupled with insistence upon the Open Door principle of equal opportunity for United States companies in new areas." That is a fair characterization of the famous principle of the "Open Door."

As I mentioned before, the "absolute position presently obtaining" in Central America, and rapidly expanding at the time in the Middle East, was based not only on overwhelming U.S. economic and military power but also on effective state intervention at the expense of rivals such as Britain. But once the "absolute position" has been achieved, "free competition" must be defended "everywhere."

In some cases, fascist powers have been enemies, in other cases, friends, depending on the role they play with regard to the Fifth Freedom. Thus in Asia, fascist Japan became an enemy in the 1930s as it responded to its effective exclusion from the imperial systems (British, Dutch, U.S.) by creating a "co-prosperity sphere" in East Asia to which U.S. access would be limited. In contrast, the semi-fascist Marcos dictatorship installed in 1972 with U.S. backing in the Philippines was a friend, and remained so until Marcos could no longer be maintained, because it firmly defended the Fifth Freedom, reversing measures that might have led to Philippine control over their own land and resources under a capitalist democracy.

The major enemy, however, is always the indigenous population, which has an unfortunate tendency to succumb to strange and unacceptable ideas about using their resources for their own purposes. They must therefore be taught regular lessons in obedience to thwart any such evil designs. Thus in Southeast Asia in the post-World War II period, national movements arose that did not comprehend the conceptions developed by State Department planners, who explained in internal documents that the region was "to fulfill its major function as a source of raw materials and a market for Japan and Western Europe." The more general plan was that East Asia and Western Europe were to be reconstructed as regional groupings dominated by Japan and Germany, their "natural leaders," within the overarching U.S.-dominated system of world order. The effort to tame the enemies of "stability" and "order" in Indochina, who rejected their assigned "function," was to become a major theme of postwar history.

Others too fail to understand their function in the global system, and must be properly disciplined. In the terminology of U.S. political theology, they are "Communists," a broad-ranging concept that has little relation to social, political or economic doctrines but a great deal to do with a proper understanding of one's duties and

function in the global system. A prestigious study group of the
Woodrow Wilson Foundation and the National Planning Association in 1955 explained the meaning of the term "Communist" can-
didly and accurately: the primary threat of "Communism," the
study observed, is the economic transformation of the Communist
powers "in ways which reduce their willingness and ability to complement the industrial economies of the West"—where "West" includes Japanese capitalism, and it is understood that these
industrial capitalist economies are to remain firmly within the U.S.-
managed "overall framework of order," in Kissinger's phrase. This
is a good definition of the term "Communism" as it is actually used
in U.S. political discourse. In brief, the "Communists" are those
who attempt to use their resources for their own purposes, thus interfering with the right to rob and to exploit, the central doctrine
of foreign policy. Naturally, the U.S. is consistently "anti-Commu-
nist," while only selectively anti-fascist.

The first principle of U.S. foreign policy, then, is to ensure a
favorable global environment for U.S.-based industry, commerce,
agribusiness and finance. In the Third World, its primary concern
is the defense of the Fifth Freedom from various enemies, primarily indigenous. What is called "national security policy" is ori-
ented to the same ends. In the fourth lecture, I will turn to the
question of just what national security policy is. For the moment,
let me just say what it is not: its primary concern is not the security of the United Stares or its allies, except in the sense of se-
curing the Fifth Freedom.

A second and related central principle is that an ideological
system must be constructed to ensure that the population remains
passive, ignorant and apathetic, and that none of these matters
are understood among the educated, articulate and politically active classes in the United States or, indeed, in the world in general.
Recall that in the operative sense of the term "democracy," these
minority elements are to dominate the "democratic process"—the

political system, the media, the educational system—as indeed they do, serving the interests of those who own and manage U.S. society and privileged groups more generally. A threat to this system of elite domination is a threat to "democracy," which must be overcome, by force if necessary.

These two basic principles are well supported in the documentary record of planning and discussion, which is available to us to quite a remarkable degree in the United States, a society that is extremely open by world standards. More important, they are very well supported by the evolving record of history.

Before proceeding, we should be clear about the fact that nothing in this record is unique to the United States. Consider Great Britain, which led the industrial revolution once it had effectively destroyed Indian cottage industry and passed beyond piracy (a major enterprise of the British colonists in America as well) to the point where it could exploit for its own ends the resources of India, the West Indies, and other regions. As it became the world-dominant power in the 19th century, Britain discovered the virtues of free trade, and maintained its devotion to these elevated principles as long as it was in a position to fare quite well in the competition. By the 1920s, this was no longer possible, and Britain moved to close the empire to free penetration by others, notably Japan, barred from free commercial relations with the British imperial system by the high tariffs imposed at the 1932 Ottawa conference. This was one of the steps that led to World War II. Throughout, the British solemnly bore "the White Man's Burden," just as the French conducted their impressive "civilizing mission": robbing, enslaving, destroying, leaving misery and starvation in their wake. The United States has resorted to protectionist measures and state intervention in the domestic and international economy throughout its history, but like Britain, has extolled the principles of free trade and the Open Door in circumstances when these proved serviceable to the business interests that control state policy. Its devotion to freedom and democracy is apparent for all to see in Central America and elsewhere, a matter to which we return.

As for the second contemporary superpower, its domestic system of control is quite different, and accordingly it plays a different role in world affairs. It is not a major factor in the exploitation and robbery of the Third World, but its ruling military-bureaucratic elite controls the internal empire and the satellites by the use or threat of violence, sends its armies to ravage neighboring countries when this is deemed necessary, and happily consorts with the worst monsters in the international arena, for example, Argentina under the neo-Nazi generals, for whom the USSR served as one of the leading trading partners.

Rather generally, throughout history, the power of some state provides a fair measure of its external violence and the hypocrisy of its doctrinal system, which can be trusted to portray the exercise of state power in terms of unsurpassed nobility and inspiring dedication to the highest moral values. Within the ideological system, it is permissible, even meritorious, to record "errors" and "failures" in pursuit of these noble objectives, but not to expose their systematic patterns and to trace these "blunders" to the conscious planning that regularly underlies them or to their roots in the pattern of privilege and domination in the domestic society.

With these general remarks behind us, let us turn to the topic at hand, considering first U.S. foreign policy, particularly with regard to the Third World, and turning to national security policy and the domestic scene later on.

From its earliest days, the United States had wide-ranging imperial aspirations. In 1754, Benjamin Franklin, a leading spokesman for Enlightenment values, defined "the father of his nation" as the man who "removes the Natives to give his own people Room." And indeed, from the origins of the colonial settlement through the 19th century, the native population was removed or destroyed through massacre, crop destruction, robbery and cheating, or expulsion, always with the highest motives, always in self-defense. In 1831, Alexis de Tocqueville observed "the triumphal march of civilization across the desert" as "in the middle of the winter," when the "cold was unusually severe," "three or four thousand soldiers drive before them the wandering races of the aborigines," who "brought in their train the wounded and the sick, with children newly born and old men on the verge of death," a "solemn spectacle" that would never fade from his memory. He was particularly impressed by the way the pioneers could deprive Indians of their rights and exterminate them "with singular felicity, tranquilly, legally, philanthropically, without shedding blood, and without violating a single great principle of morality in the eyes of the world." It was impossible to destroy people with "more respect for the laws of humanity," he observed.

Half a century earlier, the Founding Fathers, in their bill of indictment in the Declaration of Independence, had accused the King of England of inciting against the suffering colonies "the merciless Indian Savages, whose known rule of warfare, is an undistinguished destruction of all ages, sexes and conditions." They were referring to the response of the native population to the genocidal assaults launched against them by the saintly Puritans and other merciless European savages who had taught the Indians that warfare, European-style, is a program of mass extermination of women and children; George Washington was soon to teach the same lesson to the Iroquois as he sent his forces to destroy their society and civilization, quite advanced by the standards of the era, in 1779. Rarely have hypocrisy and moral cowardice been so explicit, and admired with such reverence for centuries. It was, in fact, not until the 1960s, when the popular movements in the United Stares substantially raised the moral and intellectual level of the country—the major reason why they are so reviled and despised by the educated classes—that it became possible to face this history with a degree of honesty.

In 1786, Thomas Jefferson described "our confederacy" as "the nest, from which all America, North and South, is to be peopled." It is just as well, he felt, that the continent should be in the hands of the Spanish throne until "our population can be sufficiently advanced to gain it from them piece by piece." John Quincy Adams, while formulating the thinking that led to the Monroe Doctrine, described "our proper dominion" as "the continent of North America." This is the law of nature, he explained. The law of nature had wide application. Adams invoked it again in reference to China's vain attempt to bar opium imports from India, which led to the Opium Wars, as Britain resorted to violence to overcome China's resistance to the noble principles of free trade that would have excluded Britain from the China market by blocking the major export it could offer to China. China's effort to block the import of opium was contrary to the law of nature, Adams explained. The Chinese exclusion policy is "an enormous outrage upon the rights of human nature, and upon the first principles of the rights of nations." It is immoral, because it violates the Christian principle of "love thy neighbor"—and interferes with commerce. The American Board of Missions described the Opium Wars as "not so much an opium or an English affair, as the result of a great design of Providence to make the wickedness of man subserve his purposes of mercy towards China, in breaking through her wall of exclusion, and bringing the empire into more immediate contact with western and christian nations." Fortunately, God has always been on the side of commercial advantage, a great good fortune for a nation so deeply imbued with religious values as the United States.

Turning to more recent times, Woodrow Wilson outlined "our peculiar duty": to teach colonial peoples "order and self-control" and "the drill and habit of law and obedience"—in practice, obe-

dience to our right to rob them and exploit them. In a private
paper, he explained the role of state power in this endeavor:

> Since trade ignores national boundaries and the manufacturer
> insists on having the world as a market, the flag of his nation
> must follow him, and the doors of the nations which are closed
> against him must be battered down. Concessions obtained by
> financiers must be safeguarded by ministers of state, even if the
> sovereignty of unwilling nations be outraged in the process.
> Colonies must be obtained or planted, in order that no useful
> corner of the world may be overlooked or left unused.

Used by us, of course, not by the colonized peoples. These secret
words express the true meaning of the Wilsonian ideals of freedom
and self-determination, much extolled by Western intellectuals.

When he became President a few years later, Wilson was in a
position to implement his doctrine of self-determination, as he did
by invading Mexico and Hispaniola (Haiti and the Dominican Republic), where his warriors murdered and destroyed, reestablished
virtual slavery, demolished the political system, and placed the
countries firmly in the hands of U.S. investors. His Secretary of
State, Robert Lansing, explained the meaning of the Monroe Doctrine in a memorandum that Wilson thought it would be "impolitic"
to issue publicly, though he found its argument "unanswerable":

> In its advocacy of the Monroe Doctrine the United States con-
> siders its own interests. The integrity of other American na-
> tions is an incident, not an end. While this may seem based on
> selfishness alone, the author of the Doctrine had no higher or
> more generous motive in its declaration.

The major problem, Lansing went on, is to exclude European
control over "American territory and its institutions through financial as well as other means." Wilson's practice conformed to
this principle, for example, by excluding Britain from Central
American oil concessions, as I mentioned earlier. The major
change after World War II is that the United States was then in

a position to apply these principles over a broader range; and, of course, the Evil Empire from which it had to defend itself was no longer the Huns (as in Hispaniola, according to official doctrine) or the British. Throughout, of course, the real enemy remains unchanged: the indigenous population, never able to comprehend properly that its "function" is to serve the needs of the privileged.

The documentary record yields ample treasures of a similar nature, but instead of reviewing it further, let us move directly to the current era, to the global system established by World War II.

The U.S. emerged from the war in a position of global dominance with few if any historical parallels. Its industrial rivals had been destroyed or severely weakened, while U.S. industrial production almost quadrupled during the wartime years; long before, the U.S. had become the world's leading industrial power by a large margin. The U.S. literally had about one-half of the world's wealth as the war ended. In military power, it reigned supreme. It faced no enemies in the Western Hemisphere. It controlled both oceans, and large areas beyond. Rarely if ever has a state enjoyed such power and security from threat.

The elite groups that control the state understood the situation very well, and were determined to keep things that way. There was, of course, a range of opinion. At the hard-line extreme we have such documents as National Security Council Memorandum 68 (NSC-68) of 1950, written just before the Korean war by Paul Nitze and adopted as state policy shortly after, one of the crucial documents of modern history. NSC-68 called for a rollback strategy aiming "to hasten the decay of the Soviet system" from within and to "foster the seeds of destruction within the Soviet system" by a variety of covert and other means that would enable the U.S. to "negotiate a settlement with the Soviet Union (or a successor state or states)." Covert means at the time included sending supplies and agents to armies fighting within the USSR and Eastern Europe that had been encouraged by Hitler;

placing West German espionage services under the control of Reinhard Gehlen, who had headed Nazi military intelligence on the Eastern front; recruiting Nazi war criminals to assist in the general postwar project of destroying the anti-fascist resistance, often in favor of Nazi and Japanese collaborators; and so on. At the other extreme we find the doves, such as George Kennan, who headed the State Department Planning Staff until 1950, when he was removed in favor of Nitze, being regarded as not sufficiently rough-minded for this harsh world. Kennan's views were succinctly expressed in Policy Planning Study (PPS) 23 of February 1948:

> ...we have about 50% of the world's wealth, but only 6.3% of its population. . . . In this situation, we cannot fail to be the object of envy and resentment. Our real task in the coming period is to devise a pattern of relationships which will permit us to maintain this position of disparity without positive detriment to our national security. To do so, we will have to dispense with all sentimentality and day-dreaming; and our attention will have to be concentrated everywhere on our immediate national objectives. We need not deceive ourselves that we can afford today the luxury of altruism and world-benefaction. . . . We should cease to talk about vague and—for the Far East— unreal objectives such as human rights, the raising of the living standards, and democratization. The day is not far off when we are going to have to deal in straight power concepts. The less we are then hampered by idealistic slogans, the better.

This of course is a Top Secret document. To pacify the public, and in particular the intellectual elites, it is constantly necessary to trumpet "idealistic slogans," in accordance with the principles of the ideological system which I mentioned earlier and which are richly illustrated in the media, journals of opinion, school texts, scholarly record, and productions of intellectuals quite generally, over a very broad range.

It might be noted, incidentally, that material of this sort is generally excluded from the record of scholarship and memoirs.

In particular, Kennan's conceptions, as illustrated in the secret planning documents, arc studiously ignored, not only in his memoirs but also in the extensive scholarship concerning Kennan and the "containment policy." With rare exceptions, this literature holds that Kennan had no geopolitical vision, apart from some vague and idealistic slogans, scrupulously avoiding the very clear and articulate geopolitical vision of this influential figure.

These particular prescriptions referred to the Far East, but the United States is a global power, and the same principles apply elsewhere, as Kennan and others explained. Thus, in a briefing for Latin American ambassadors in 1950, Kennan observed that a major concern of American foreign policy must be "The protection of our raw materials"—in fact, more broadly, the material and human resources that are "ours" by right. To protect our resources, we must combat a dangerous heresy which, as U.S. intelligence noted, had been spreading through Latin America: "the wide acceptance of the idea that the government has direct responsibility for the welfare of the people," what is called "Communism," whatever the political commitments of its advocates, in U.S. political theology.

Kennan went on to explain the means that we must use against our enemies who fall prey to the heresy that threatens our resources in their lands:

> The final answer might be an unpleasant one, but. . .we should not hesitate before police repression by the local government. This is not shameful since the Communists are essentially traitors. . .It is better to have a strong regime in power than a liberal government if it is indulgent and relaxed and penetrated by Communists.

Here the term "Communist" must be understood in the usual sense of U.S. political theology, already discussed.

According to John Loftus, who investigated these matters for the U.S. Justice Department, the covert operations I mentioned earlier within the Soviet Union and Eastern Europe were run from the office of George Kennan in the State Department. The comments I quoted earlier on the "function" of Southeast Asia also derive from Kennan's Policy Planning Staff, which had considerable influence in determining the contours of the postwar world, including the measures undertaken in the late 1940s to construct regional systems under the U.S. aegis in Asia and Europe organized around their "natural leaders," Japan and Germany. In the case of Japan, Kennan and his staff were instrumental in devising the "reverse course" of 1947, which terminated General Douglas McArthur's steps towards democratizing Japan. The "reverse course" effectively curbed Japanese labor and reestablished "democracy" in the preferred sense of the term: firm control by business interests in a conservative Japan which, it was expected, would become a regional leader within a broader U.S.-dominated global system. The thought that Japan might become a serious competitor was then too exotic to be considered. As late as the early 1960s, the Kennedy Administration was still concerned with finding means to ensure Japan's viability, finally established by the Vietnam war, costly to the U.S. but highly beneficial to the Japanese economy, as the Korean war had been.

In Europe, the parallel program was the Marshall Plan, in part an export promotion program for U.S. industry, in part a program to promote economic recovery within a regional system subordinated to global U.S. interests. A major concern was to eliminate the danger of independent political developments that might have led to a form of national capitalism, or even worse, that might have given undue influence to mass-based socialist movements which had considerable prestige because of their central role in the anti-fascist resistance.

The views of Nitze and Kennan demarcate fairly well the spectrum of opinion among planners. There is no space here to review the documentary record, but it falls quite closely within this spectrum, though one can find some qualifications. One influential study of April 1947 observed that U.S. aid should be restricted to "countries of primary strategic importance to the United States . . . , excepting in those rare instances which present an opportunity for the United States to gain world wide approbation by an act strikingly humanitarian" (Joint Chiefs of Staff 1769/1), in which case, the act will provide grist for the mills of the commissars. In accordance with this qualification, for example, Secretary of State Dean Acheson and influential U.S. Senators agreed in 1950 "that should starvation break out in mainland China the United States should give a little food aid—not enough to alleviate the starvation, but enough for a psychological warfare advantage," as Stephen Shalom documents in an important study of neo-colonialism.

As I have already mentioned, such a stance is of course not unique to the United States, nor did it arise in the postwar period, though the scope of application of the guiding principles of foreign policy extended worldwide in accordance with the vast expansion of U.S. power.

George Kennan's lucid presentation of U.S. foreign policy goals did not emerge from a vacuum. It reflected a broader geopolitical analysis that had been developed by elite groups during the war. Study groups of the Council on Foreign Relations (a major channel for business influence on foreign policy) and the State Department formulated the concept of what they called the "Grand Area," a region that should be subordinated to the needs of the American economy and that was to include at a minimum the Western Hemisphere, the Far East, and the former British empire. It was to be expanded to a global system to the extent possible, surely including Western Europe and the incomparable energy reserves of the Middle East, then passing into American hands. This documentary record of high-level planning is also excluded from sanitized history. These guiding geopolitical conceptions explain a good deal of what has been happening in the world; if they are not understood, what takes place will appear to be a series of random errors, confusions and inconsistencies, traceable to the failings of a political leadership that is, in fact, succeeding brilliantly in its assigned tasks, despite the occasional failures that are inevitable in a complex world.

In a major scholarly analysis of U.S. security policy based in part on recently released documents, Melvyn Leffler observes that as World War II ended, "the American conception of national security . . . included a strategic sphere of influence within the Western Hemisphere [from which others, crucially Europe, were to be excluded, and where "strategic influence" includes economic control], domination of the Atlantic and Pacific oceans, an extensive system of outlying bases to enlarge the strategic frontier and project American power, an even more extensive system of transit rights to facilitate the conversion of commercial air bases to military use, access to the resources and markets of most of Eurasia, denial of these resources to a prospective enemy, and the maintenance of nuclear superiority. "This strategic conception helps explain "the dynamics of the Cold War after 1948," Leffler comments. It was an expansive vision, consistent with the awesome power of the United States at the time.

In subsequent years, the views expressed by early postwar planners were repeatedly developed with reference to particular areas. In connection with Latin America, after the successful overthrow of Guatemalan democracy in 1954 the National Security Council explained the central U.S. objectives in the Top Secret memorandum NSC 5432, August 18, 1954, entitled "U.S. Policy Toward Latin America." This replaced NSC 5419/1, entitled "U.S. Policy in the Event of Guatemalan Aggression in Latin America." Now that U.S. aggression had eliminated the danger of independent Guatemalan capitalist democracy, it was unnecessary to contemplate ways to respond to the grave threat of

Guatemalan aggression, before which the hemisphere had been quaking in terror. Here we see illustrated the traditional device of accusing the target of aggression of being the perpetrator of the planned crime, so that we must attack it in self-defense, as when Hitler accused Czechoslovakia and Poland of planning aggression against Germany in concert with the great powers encircling peace-loving Germany.

With the threat of Guatemalan aggression successfully removed, the U.S. could turn to ensuring "Increased Stability and Economic Development," crucially, "encouraging a climate conducive to private investment." The document piously recognizes "the sovereign right of Latin American countries to undertake such economic measures as they believe are best adapted to their own conditions," but the U.S. nevertheless should "encourage them to base their economies on a system of private enterprise, and, as essential thereto, to create a political and economic climate conducive to private investment of both domestic and foreign capital," by means it proceeds to elaborate, including guarantees for the "Opportunity to earn and in the case of foreign capital to repatriate a reasonable return." The goal expressed throughout is to foster export-oriented economic development with U.S. corporations firmly in command. It goes unsaid, as redundant, that if the "sovereign" countries of Latin America are reluctant to accept U.S. advice, other measures of "encouragement" may be necessary, as had just been demonstrated in Guatemala.

The primary concern of U.S. policy is stated plainly in the opening words of the document:

> There is a trend in Latin America toward nationalistic regimes maintained in large part by appeals to the masses of the population. Concurrently, there is an increasing popular demand for immediate improvement in the low living standards of the masses, with the result that most Latin American governments are under intense domestic political pressures to increase production and to diversify their economics [sic].

Plainly this will never do. Therefore, while giving token recognition to "the importance of bettering conditions for the general population," the U.S. must take "a realistic and constructive approach" which recognizes that it "is essential to arrest the drift in the area toward radical and nationalistic regimes." "The growth of nationalism," the memorandum continues, "is facilitated by historic anti-U.S. prejudices and exploited by Communists." U.S. assistance is required to block "Communist intervention and subversion," exploiting such "prejudice." It is naturally taken for granted, as in journalism and much of scholarship, that critical attitudes towards Big Brother can only be "prejudice," and since those who exploit such prejudice are "Communists" by definition (whatever their social and political commitments), it is unnecessary to provide evidence to support the fears over "Communist intervention and subversion."

The memorandum goes on to emphasize the need for "Hemisphere solidarity in support of our world policies"; "the reduction and elimination of the menace of internal Communist or other anti-U.S. subversion" (my emphasis: note that a touch of realism intrudes at this point); "Adequate production in Latin America of, and access by the United States to, raw materials essential to U.S. security" (a broad category, as the record shows); and "The ultimate standardization of Latin American military organization, training, doctrine and equipment along U.S. lines." The latter is crucial, since to arrest the dangerous trend towards nationalism accompanied by concern for the domestic population, it will be necessary to make use of domestic military forces, such as the National Guards established after Marine intervention in the Dominican Republic, Nicaragua and elsewhere—or the direct use of U.S. force, if these domestic means of "encouragement" do not suffice.

Note that the insistence on "individual and collective action against Communist or other anti-U.S. subversion or intervention in any American state" anticipates the "Brezhnev Doctrine" enunciated in 1968 by Soviet leader Leonid Brezhnev with regard to Eastern Europe, a doctrine bitterly condemned as the ultimate proof of the viciousness of the Evil Empire and its menace to civilization. Just prior to the 1954 invasion of Guatemala from Nicaragua and Honduras (including bombing of the capital by the U.S. air force), the U.S. had pressured the foreign ministers of the Latin American states "to achieve maximum agreement among the American Republics upon a clear-cut and unmistakable policy determination against the intervention of international communism in the hemisphere, recognizing the continuing threat which it poses to their peace and security and declaring their intention to take effective measures, individually and collectively, to combat it," so we read in the State Department *Bulletin*, April 26, 1954. The *Bulletin* goes on to record the agreement of the Inter-American Conference that "the domination or control of the political institutions of any American State by the international communist movement, extending to this hemisphere the political system of an extracontinental power, would constitute a threat to the sovereignty and political independence of the American States, endangering the peace of America. . . ." The Kennedy-Johnson liberals expanded this doctrine further in connection with Cuba and the Dominican Republic, effectively establishing the principle that sovereignty in the Western Hemisphere is limited by the ideological principles determined by the hemispheric superpower; governments that deviate from these principles are guilty of "aggression," and the U.S. may invade and overthrow them in "self-defense." As President Lyndon Johnson explained when he sent the Marines to the Dominican Republic, "American nations cannot, must not, and will not permit the establishment of another Communist government in the Western Hemisphere" (May 2, 1965)—here the "Communist government" was the constitutional government headed by the elected President Juan Bosch, a Kennedy-style democrat whose independence had incurred the wrath of the United States. Throughout, it is assumed that "alien ideologies" are intolerable in the Western Hemisphere, and as the guardian of virtue, the U.S. has the right to "defend " the hemisphere against them by subversion or outright force.

NSC 5432 proceeds to outline the steps required to integrate the Latin American military within the U.S. system of hemispheric "encouragement": "Increase the quotas of qualified Latin American personnel for training in U.S. Armed Forces schools and training centers," including the military academies; "Foster closer relations between Latin American and U.S. military personnel in order to increase the understanding of, and orientation toward, U.S. objectives on the part of the Latin American military, recognizing that the military establishments of most Latin American states play an influential role in government"; "Seek ultimate military standardization, along U.S. lines, of the organization, training, doctrine and equipment of Latin American armed forces, countering trends toward the establishment of European military missions in Latin America" and ensuring that U.S. equipment will be used. Notice that these moves to effectively integrate the Latin American military within the U.S. military command structure are directed against both of our historic enemies in Latin America: Europe, and the indigenous population.

I will return in lecture three to some of the ways in which these ideas were developed and applied in Latin America, in particular, to the fateful decision of the Kennedy liberals to shift the mission of the Latin American military from "hemispheric defense" to "internal security." A secret study by Robert McNamara's Defense Department (June 11, 1965) picks up the themes just reviewed after these steps had been taken. This memorandum, entitled "Study of U.S. Policy Toward Latin American Military Forces," observes that "U.S. policies toward the Latin American military have,

on the whole, been effective in attaining the goals set for them. . . ,"
in particular, "establishing predominant U.S. military influence"
and "improving internal security capabilities." "The primary role of
these military forces is to protect the sovereignty of their nations,"
but, the study explains, this obligation has a special meaning in
"the Latin American cultural environment": namely, in order to
"protect the sovereignty of their nations," the Latin American military must be prepared to act "to remove government leaders from
office whenever, in the judgment of the military, the conduct of
these leaders is injurious to the welfare of the nation." With U.S.
control firmly established and the Latin American military having
mastered "the understanding of, and orientation toward, U.S. objectives," we can be assured that "the judgment of the military" will
reflect the preferences of Big Brother as they pursue their "primary
role," guaranteeing that "democracy" will function within the limits
established by the Ruler of the Hemisphere.

The study also outlines the roots of the "U.S. political interest in Latin America" in conventional terms:

> Oldest is the military one which springs from the geographical
> proximity of Latin America to the continental U.S., from the
> importance of the Panama canal as a traffic artery and, partic-
> ularly during the World War II period, from the strategic raw
> materials which the area can supply. Somewhat younger, al-
> though possibly stronger, is the economic root whose central
> fiber is the $9 billion of private U.S. investment in the area and
> the related fact that U.S. trade with Latin America is nearly
> $7 billion annually.

A major priority, then, is "to protect and promote American
investment and trade" as well as "to foster concerted diplomatic
action and support of U.S. cold war positions" while improving
"the military contribution to internal security." The tasks are addressed in some detail on a country-by-country basis.

The document stresses throughout the dangers of "nationalism" and "neutralism," which might "give fresh impetus to endemic

anti-Americanism" including "rejection of U.S. counsel" and inter-ference with U.S. economic interests. As committed Marxists, the planners are particularly concerned that "The contemporary fer-ment in Latin America is giving rise to a revolutionary struggle for power among major groups which constitute the present class structure"; naturally U.S. elites must position themselves properly to determine the outcome of this class struggle. Hence the impor-tance of ensuring control over the internal security forces, which "as a whole are probably the least anti-American of any political group in Latin America" as a result of the effectiveness of the poli-cies of assuring the "predominant influence" of the U.S. over this "political group." The emphasis throughout is on enabling these forces to preserve "order," in accord with the policy initiated in 1961-62, when the U.S. "began furnishing equipment and training specifically identified as intended for internal security," the major contribution of Kennedy liberalism to Latin America. There are certain impediments, such as the unfortunate fact that the legal systems in Latin American countries "require courts to free pris-oners, even notorious guerrillas, without regard for the circum-stances of their capture, unless witnesses can testify they actually saw the accused commit the crime with which he is charged" and "the reluctance of governments to establish bilateral or multilateral arrangements for the control of travelers," as achieved in the U.S. through legislation to bar "subversives" from the Land of the Free. But these "handicaps" can be overcome, and were, by such meth-ods as "disappearance," torture, or large-scale slaughter under U.S. auspices. As we have seen, State Department dove George Kennan had observed much earlier that "we should not hesitate before po-lice repression by the local government" and that "It is better to have a strong regime in power than a liberal government if it is in-dulgent and relaxed and penetrated by Communists."

It was not only the existing opportunities for exploitation, bur the potential ones that planners had to consider, as they devoted themselves to ensuring that the region would remain firmly under U.S. domination to the maximum extent possible, including the potential supply of cheap labor for assembly and manufacturing. There is rich documentation of a similar nature with regard to Southeast Asia, which I have discussed elsewhere. The leading concepts are not at all surprising, nor should we be surprised that they were not only formulated—generally in secret, but sometimes publicly—but more important, applied in regular and systematic practice.

I would like to turn now to the question of what all this has meant for the world since World War II. Let us consider several elements of the world system that has emerged.

Let us begin with the Third World, which was to be incorporated within the Grand Area so that its various regions could "fulfill their functions." I will return to some of the many problems that arose in carrying out this task. A rough measure of these problems is given by a 1983 review by Ruth Sivard of major military conflicts since World War II, conducted under the auspices of the Institute of World Order, the Rockefeller Foundation, and other similarly respectable institutions. She estimates that there were about 125 major conflicts, 95% of them in the Third World, in most cases involving foreign forces, with "western powers accounting for 79% of the interventions, communist for 6%." The toll has been enormous. In Indochina alone, there may have been close to 4 million killed in the course of the French and American wars of aggression, while 3 countries were left in ruins.* In Afghanistan, estimates of the death toll caused by the Soviet ag-

---

*Estimates of casualties in Third World countries are always very rough approximations, and those that appear in the journalistic and scholarly literature should always be understood as such. There is also a strong tendency, which I have documented elsewhere, to exaggerate the crimes of enemies and minimize those of one's own state or clients. Here and below, estimates are the most reliable I have been able to find. See the sources in the bibliographical note for references.

gression range from one-half million to a million, and there has been vast destruction. In Indonesia, one-half to a million people were slaughtered in four months, mostly landless peasants, after a military coup backed (and possibly inspired) by the United States in 1965, an operation much lauded by Western (including liberal) opinion and offered as a justification for the American war in Indochina, which had provided a "shield" behind which the Indonesian generals were encouraged to carry out this necessary task of purging their society of dangerous elements and opening it to Western robbery, with the destruction of the mass-based Communist Party. Since 1975, some 200,000 people have been killed in East Timor in the course of an Indonesian invasion carried out with the crucial military and diplomatic support of the United States and its allies, a massacre that probably achieves the postwar record of slaughter, relative to the population. In Central America, close to 200,000 people have been killed since 1978, many with hideous torture and mutilation, by U.S. client governments with the crucial support of the United States and its allies. These are only a few examples. These Third World conflicts have repeatedly brought the superpowers close to confrontation, primarily in the Middle East. This threat is very real, and persists, a matter that I want to consider in the fourth lecture.

These estimates understate the lethal consequences of U.S. intervention in the Third World. When we try to assess the crimes of the Pol Pot regime, we rightly consider not only actual killing, but also the effect of harsh and brutal policies that led to death from malnutrition, the conditions of life and labor, lack of health facilities, and so on. No similar estimate has been attempted of the impact of U.S. policies in the Third World, and I will not try to speculate here on the scale of these much larger atrocities. Quite often in areas of predominant U.S. influence such as Latin America, there has been statistical growth in the course of "economic miracles" while much of the population starves as croplands are devoted to exports for the benefit of U.S. agribusiness and local elites. The U.S. is the world's largest food importer, primarily from the Third World, while its massive food exports go primarily to advanced industrial societies, or for such projects as producing beef for export to U.S. markets, replacing local subsistence agriculture. Kennedy's Alliance for Progress gave a major impetus to these destructive—indeed, if we were honest, murderous—developments, a topic to which I will return in the third lecture, along with the relation between these models of development and the terror-and-torture states that are their natural concomitant.

Let us turn our attention now to Europe and to early postwar programs to consolidate the Grand Area.

In Europe, the Soviet Union established its control over the satellite countries after World War II while the United States incorporated Western and Southern Europe within the Grand Area. Europe posed problems for U.S. planners, but Soviet aggression was considered a remote eventuality, contrary to much propaganda then and since. In the late 1940s, U.S. intelligence did not take this possibility seriously. They estimated that it would take the USSR 15 years to overcome wartime losses in manpower and industry and that the USSR would not reach the pre-World War II levels of the United States for 15 to 20 years, even with "Herculean efforts." The most detailed current stud y of the postwar Soviet army, by the American scholar Michael Evangelista, indicates that even in numerical terms, Western forces matched those of the Soviet Union in Europe, putting aside their cohesion and morale, their far more advanced technical level and economic base, and the fact that Soviet forces were engaged in reconstruction of large areas devastated by the Nazi attack, which had concentrated its fury primarily on the Eastern front.

Western planners were concerned over "the loss of Europe," but not to Soviet military conquest. Rather, as the CIA warned in 1947, "the greatest danger to the security of the United States is the possibility of economic collapse in Western Europe and the consequent accession to power of Communist elements." Similarly, Dean Acheson, while attempting successfully to mobilize Congressional support for intervention in Greece under the Truman Doctrine, warned that "Like apples in a barrel infected by one rotten one, the corruption of Greece would infect Iran and all to the east" and would "carry infection" to Asia Minor, Egypt and Africa, as well as to Italy and France, which were "threatened" by large Communist parties. We return to the interesting and quite characteristic imagery, and its meaning, bur we see again that the threat in Europe was democratic politics, a particularly serious matter because of the prestige of the anti-Nazi resistance, much of it inspired by a vision of radical democracy, and including significant socialist and Communist elements.

The primary concern had been formulated by South African Prime Minister Jan Christiaan Smuts, one of Winston Churchill's most trusted advisers, who warned Churchill in 1943, with regard to southern Europe, that "with politics let loose among those peoples, we may have a wave of disorder and wholesale Communism set going all over those parts of Europe." Neither so-called "Communism," nor socialism, nor radical democracy, nor national capitalism that might strike an independent course was tolerable. These were the threats that had to be confronted, not Soviet aggression.

In the next lecture I will discuss the way these threats were addressed, and will turn to other aspects of the global order constructed after World War II.

LECTURE 2

Containing Internal Aggression

In the last lecture, I reviewed some of the documentary record of high level U.S. planning. From this record, we see that there is indeed a spectrum of opinion, but a very narrow one. Disagreements are mainly over tactical issues, over how best to achieve goals that are accepted with few questions and little need for discussion, since they are so widely shared among the elite groups that take an active part in the political system, that staff the executive branch of the government, and that provide the extragovernmental framework that sets the conditions within which state policy is formulated and executed.

The central concern, with regard to the Third World, is to defend the right to rob and to exploit, to protect "our" raw materials. More generally, the concern is to maintain the Grand Area subordinated to the needs of U.S. elites and to ensure that other powers are limited to their "regional interests" within the "overall framework of order" maintained and controlled by the United States. In the words of George Kennan, the leading dove among early postwar planners, we must put aside "vague and . . . unreal objectives such as human rights, the raising of the living standards, and democratization," and be prepared to use violence if necessary to achieve our objectives, not "hampered by idealistic slogans."

The main enemy is the indigenous population who attempt to steal *our* resources that happen to be in *their* countries, who are concerned with vague and idealistic objectives such as human rights, the raising of the living standards, and democratization, and who, in their backwardness and folly, find it difficult to understand that their "function" is to "complement the industrial economies of the West" (including Japan) and to serve the needs of the privileged groups that dominate these societies. The major danger posed by these indigenous enemies is that unless they are stopped in time, they may spread the virus of independence, freedom, and concern for human welfare, infecting regions beyond; they must be prevented from turning their societies into rotten apples, which may infect the barrel, threatening the stability of the Grand Area. As other planners put it, the United States must "prevent the rot from spreading." It must prevent what is sometimes—on different assumptions as to what is right and just—called "the threat of a good example." The threat of rot and infection is a serious one, which requires serious measures, violence if necessary, always presented as the defense of the highest values, in the classic manner.

The main lines of thinking are expressed clearly in Top Secret documents and planning studies, and sometimes in public statements as well, but it is missing from political analysis, journalism, or even most of scholarship, in accordance with the second major principle of policy: the ideological system too must serve its "function," namely, to ensure the required level of ignorance and apathy on the part of the general population as well as among politically active elites, except, of course, for those engaged not just in ideological control but also in serious planning and execution of policy.

I then began to discuss the world system that has developed since World War II, concentrating on the U.S. role, as I will do throughout these lectures. I ended the last lecture with a few remarks on the Third World and on post-World War II Europe and the problems it posed for Grand Area planning: not the threat of Soviet aggression, but the threat of economic collapse and democratic politics, which might lead to forms of social and economic development outside of the U.S.-dominated framework of world order.

To overcome these threats, the U.S. undertook the Marshall Plan and similar programs, which, as noted earlier, also served as critically important subsidies to U.S. exporters of raw materials and manufactured goods. Meanwhile, the threat of democratic politics was met in the natural way, by undertaking a program, worldwide in scope, to destroy the anti-fascist resistance and the popular organizations associated with it, often in favor of fascists or fascist collaborators. This is, in fact, one of the major themes of early postwar history.

The pattern was set in the first area liberated, North Africa, where President Roosevelt installed in power Admiral Jean Darlan, a leading Nazi collaborator and the author of the Vichy regime's anti-Semitic laws. As U.S. forces advanced through Italy, they restored the essential structure of the fascist regime while dispersing the resistance, which had fought courageously against six Nazi divisions. In Greece, British troops entered after the Nazis had withdrawn, imposing a harsh and corrupt regime that evoked renewed resistance which Britain was unable to control in its postwar decline. The U.S. entered, replacing Britain, under the guise of Truman Doctrine rhetoric about defending "free peoples who are resisting attempted subjugation by armed minorities or by outside pressures." Meanwhile, Presidential adviser Clark Clifford happily commented in private that the Doctrine would serve as "the opening gun in a campaign to bring people up to realization that the war isn't over by any means"; and indeed, it helped set off a new era of domestic militarism and intervention abroad in the context of Cold War confrontation, Greece being

only the first target. There, the U.S. launched a murderous war
of counterinsurgency, complete with torture, political exile for
tens of thousands, reeducation camps, destruction of unions and
any independent politics, and the full panoply of means later used
in similar exercises throughout the world, placing the society
firmly in the hands of U.S. investors and local business elites,
while much of the population had to emigrate to survive. The
beneficiaries again included Nazi collaborators, while the primary
victims were the workers and peasants of the Communist-led
anti-Nazi resistance.

The successful counterinsurgency operation in Greece
served as the model for the escalation of the U.S. war against
South Vietnam in the early 1960s, as Adlai Stevenson proclaimed
at the United Nations in 1964 while explaining that in South
Vietnam, the United States was engaged in defense against "internal aggression." That is, the U.S. was undertaking the defense
of South Vietnam against the "internal aggression" of its own
population; essentially the rhetoric of the Truman Doctrine. The
Greek model was also invoked by Reagan's Central America advisor Roger Fontaine as the Reagan Administration prepared to
escalate Carter's "defense" of El Salvador against "internal aggression" there.

It might be noted that Stevenson's reputation as an outstanding spokesman for enlightened values and a leading figure of
modern liberalism is unsullied by such rhetoric as this. The doctrine that the U.S. has been engaged in defense of one or another
country against "internal aggression" is quite blandly accepted
by the educated classes in the United States, as in Europe quite
generally, a fact that provides a certain insight into the moral and
intellectual level of what passes as civilized discourse.

I will return to the Truman Doctrine in a moment, but first
it should be stressed that the pattern just described was indeed
worldwide. In Korea, the U.S. forces dispersed the local popular

government and inaugurated a brutal repression, using Japanese police and collaborators. Some 100,000 people were killed prior to what is called in the West "the Korean war," including 30-40,000 killed in the suppression of a peasant insurgency on Cheju island. Similarly in the Philippines, the anti-Japanese peasant resistance was crushed in a long and bitter war of counterinsurgency, while Japanese collaborators were restored to power. In Thailand, the U.S. vigorously supported a series of military coups that finally installed Phibun Songkhram, "the first pro-Axis dictator to regain power after the war," in the words of former CIA Thai specialist Frank Darling in his study of the United States and Thailand. The leader of the Free Thai movement that had cooperated with the United States during the war, Thailand's most prominent liberal democratic figure, was deposed by a U.S.-backed coup and ended up in Communist China. In 1954, in the secret planning to subvert the Geneva Accords that established a framework for peace in Indochina, the National Security Council proposed that Thailand be established "as the focal point of U.S. covert and psychological operations in Southeast Asia." This goal was achieved. Thailand later became the base for U.S. attacks in Indochina and a Free World bastion, complete with child slavery, horrifying exploitation of women, massive corruption, starvation and misery, and ample profits for Western investors and their Thai clients. As the Indochina war wound down, the U.S. continued to support the brutal Thai military in its successful defense against democratizing elements, as it did in the Philippines in the same period.

In Indochina, the U.S. supported France in its efforts to "defend" its former colony against the "internal aggression" of the Vietnamese nationalist movement, which had also cooperated with the U.S. during the war.

Turning to Latin America, a fascist coup in Colombia inspired by Franco's Spain aroused no *more* concern than a military coup in Venezuela or the restoration of an admirer of fascism in Panama. But the first democratic government in the history of Guatemala, modeling itself on Roosevelt's New Deal, elicited bitter U.S. antagonism and a CIA coup that turned Guatemala into a literal hell-on-earth, kept that way since with regular U.S. intervention and support, particularly under Kennedy and Johnson. The story continues through the Carter years when, contrary to what is commonly alleged, official U.S. military aid to a series of Guatemalan Himmlers never ceased and was barely below the norm, while military aid also was sent through other channels, including U.S. client regimes. Under Reagan, support for near-genocide became positively ecstatic.

The postwar pattern of marginalizing or if necessary destroying the antifascist resistance, often in favor of fascist sympathizers and collaborators, was quite a general and pervasive one. But predictably, sanitized history does not include a chapter devoted to this worldwide campaign, though one can discover the details in specialized studies dealing with one or another country. Where the facts are noted in connection with some particular country, the policy is generally described as a mistake, resulting from the ignorance or naivete of the well-meaning U.S. leadership or the confusions of the postwar era.

One aspect of this postwar project was the recruitment of Nazi war criminals such as Reinhard Gehlen, who had headed Nazi military intelligence on the Eastern Front and was given the same duties under the new West German state with close CIA supervision, or Klaus Barbie, responsible for many crimes in France and duly placed in charge of spying on the French for U.S. intelligence. The reasons were cogently explained by Barbie's superior, Col. Eugene Kolb, who noted that his "skills were badly needed"; "To our knowledge, his activities had been directed against the underground French Communist Party and Resistance, just as we in the postwar era were concerned with the German Communist Party and activities inimical to American policies in Germany." Kolb's comment is apt. The U.S. was picking up where the Nazis had left off, and it was therefore entirely natural that they should employ specialists in anti-resistance activity.

Later, when it became impossible to protect them from retribution in Europe, many of these useful folk were spirited to the United States or to Latin America, with the help of the Vatican and fascist priests. Many of them have since been engaged in terrorism, coups, the drug and armaments trade, training the apparatus of the U.S.-backed National Security States in methods of torture devised by the Gestapo, and so on. Some of their students have found their way to Central America, establishing a direct link between the Death Camps and the Death Squads, via the U.S.-SS postwar alliance.

As I've mentioned, the reasoning behind these activities was essentially that sketched out by Dean Acheson, later to become Secretary of State, in his advocacy of the Truman Doctrine before Congress. His contribution, and the general conceptions involved, merit a closer look, since they are quite central to U.S. policy planning worldwide, as a corollary to the primary principle of defense of the Fifth Freedom. The context, as described in Acheson's memoirs, was the difficulty that the Administration faced in overcoming the reluctance of Congress, reflecting the public mood, to engage in new military adventures in 1947. Acheson describes his success in overcoming this reluctance in words that merit full quotation:

> In the past eighteen months, I said, Soviet pressure on the Straits, on Iran, and on northern Greece had brought the Balkans to the point where a highly possible Soviet breakthrough might open three continents to Soviet penetration. Like apples in a barrel infected by one rotten one, the corruption of Greece would infect Iran and all to the east. It would also carry infection to Africa through Asia Minor and

Egypt, and to Europe through Italy and France, already threatened by the strongest domestic Communist parties in Western Europe.

Apart from the concern over the "threat" of democratic politics in Europe, two points merit particular notice in connection with Acheson's remarks: (1) the invocation of the Russian threat; (2) the rotten apple theory. Let us consider them in turn.

Acheson cites three examples of a "highly possible Soviet breakthrough": the Straits of the Dardanelles, Iran, and Greece. He surely knew that each of these examples was fraudulent. He was surely aware that the Soviet Union had already been rebuffed in its efforts to take part in management of the Straits, and had agreed to leave control over its only warm water access entirely in Western hands. He could also hardly have been unaware of the fact that long before, the Soviet Union had abandoned its efforts to gain a share in the exploitation of Iranian oil, on its border, leaving these riches entirely in the hands of the West. As for Greece, it is difficult to imagine that State Department intelligence had been unable to learn that Stalin was urging restraint on the Greek guerrillas (recognizing that Greece was in the U.S. sphere of influence, regarded as essentially part of the U.S.-dominated Middle East region), just as Acheson surely knew that Stalin had been instructing the Communist parties of the West to join in the reconstruction of capitalism.

Nevertheless, Acheson takes great pride in this successful exercise in deception, a fact that is as worthy of note as his concern over the dangers of democratic politics in the West. As I mentioned in the first lecture, similar concerns impelled the U.S., under prodding by Kennan and others, to reverse early steps towards democratization in Japan and place the country firmly and, it was hoped, irreversibly, under conservative business control with labor seriously weakened and few opportunities available for serious popular engagement in politics.

Acheson's success in this deception taught an important lesson for propagandists, applied many times since: when the U.S. political leadership wants to drum up support for intervention and aggression, it need only shout that the Russians are coming. Whatever the facts, this is bound to achieve the desired results. The tactic worked unfailingly until the popular movements in the 1960s somewhat improved the intellectual and moral level of U.S. society, and despite this setback, this tactic remains highly effective.

Acheson's success had further implications for policy-makers: if it is deemed necessary to arrack another country, it will be highly useful to be able to portray it as a Soviet client to reinforce the cry that the Russians are again on the march. Therefore it is useful to drive the target of aggression into the hands of the Soviet Union by embargo, threat, subversion and other measures, including pressure on allies and international agencies to withdraw assistance, so as to provide the required doctrinal basis for the planned aggression. If this goal can be achieved, it will also provide a retrospective justification for the hostile actions that were undertaken to achieve it, assuming, of course, that the media and articulate intelligentsia can be relied upon to play their assigned part in the charade—a well-founded assumption. If the goal cannot be achieved, the desired consequence can be proclaimed as fact nevertheless, with media complicity. This lesson has also been applied frequently: during the successful overthrow of capitalist democracy in Guatemala in 1954, in the case of Cuba, and with regard to Nicaragua today, among many other cases.

Liberal critics of U.S. policy, willfully blind to its obvious motives and the rich historical record, deplore the fact that the U.S. embargo will compel Nicaragua to rely on the Soviet bloc, failing to comprehend that that is precisely its aim, as in many earlier cases, for the reasons just indicated. This astonishing inability to perceive what is unfolding before their eyes is explained in part by the fact that critics within the mainstream ideological consensus

take seriously the claim that Nicaragua poses a "security threat" to
the United States. On this assumption, the Reagan Administration
must be making a foolish and inexplicable error by acting to increase the dependence of Nicaragua on the USSR by hostile measures and pressure on U.S. allies. No rational person should have
any difficulty in discerning the motive behind these quite systematic and familiar efforts: those outlined a moment ago.

We might observe in passing that the claim that Nicaragua
might endanger U.S. security makes Hitler sound sane in comparison, with his ravings about Czechoslovakia as "a dagger
pointed at the heart of Germany" and about the threat posed to
Germany by the "aggressiveness" of the Poles. If the USSR were
to warn about the threat posed by Denmark or Luxembourg to
Soviet security and the need to "contain" this dire threat, perhaps
even declaring a national emergency in the face of this grave danger, Western opinion would be rightly enraged. But when the
mainstream U.S. press and a liberal Congress, echoing the Administration, warn ominously of the need to "contain" Nicaragua,
the same thinkers nod their heads in sage assent or offer mild criticism that the threat is perhaps exaggerated. And when in May
1985, Ronald Reagan declared a "national emergency" to deal
with the "unusual and extraordinary threat to the national security
and foreign policy of the United States" posed by "the policies
and actions of the Government of Nicaragua," the reaction in
Congress and the media—and in much of Europe—was not
ridicule, but rather praise for these principled and statesmanlike
steps. All of this provides yet another indication of the level of
Western intellectual culture.

So much for the first point: Acheson's success in invoking a
fraudulent Russian threat, which became virtually a reflex in the
subsequent period, not surprisingly. Let us consider the second
point: the rotten apple theory that he expressed with such ele-
gance. This too became a staple among planners, who repeatedly

express their concern that some errant country or political move-ment or leadership will be a "contagious example" that will "in-fect" others, Kissinger's terms with reference to Allende's example of democratic socialism, which he feared would "infect" not only Latin America but also southern Europe; or that "the rot will spread" throughout Southeast Asia, perhaps engulfing Japan, the fear expressed by U.S. planners with regard to the Communist-led Vietnamese national movement.

The conventional name for the rotten apple theory is "the domino theory." This theory has two variants. One, regularly in-voked to frighten the domestic population, is that Ho Chi Minh (or whoever the current sinner may be) will climb into a canoe, conquer Indonesia, land in San Francisco, and rape your grand-mother. While it may be difficult to believe that these tales are presented seriously by the political leadership, one should not be too sure. Leaders of the calibre of Ronald Reagan may well be-lieve what they say. The same may be true of more serious polit-ical figures, for example, Lyndon Johnson, probably the most liberal President in American history and in many ways "a man of the people," who was undoubtedly speaking honestly when he warned in 1948 that unless the U.S. maintained overwhelming military superiority, it would be "a bound and throttled giant; im-potent and easy prey to any yellow dwarf with a pocket knife"; or when he said in a speech in Alaska in 1966, at the height of U.S. aggression in Vietnam, that "If we are going to have visits from any aggressors or any enemies, I would rather have that ag-gression take place out 10,000 miles from here than take place here in Anchorage," referring to the "internal aggression" of the Vietnamese against U.S. military forces in Vietnam:

> There are 3 billion people in the world [Johnson continued] and we have only 200 million of them. We are outnumbered 15 to one. If might did make right they would sweep over the United States and take what we have. We have what they want.

Difficult as it may be to believe, such sentiments are widely shared among the richest and most privileged people in the world. We need not tarry on the psychological mechanisms; what is important is that this is a fact, and one that allows much of the population to be easily aroused by jingoist rhetoric appealing to deep-seated fears.

But saner minds dismiss this version of the domino theory, and indeed it is regularly derided when some program of intervention and aggression goes awry. Nevertheless, the internal documentary record reveals that the domino theory itself is never questioned by planners; no serious question is raised about the rotten apple theory, the concern that the "virus" may be contagious. But Kissinger surely did not think that Allende was going to conquer Italy, nor did U.S. planners expect that Ho Chi Minh would conquer Japan, the "superdomino." What, then, are the mechanisms by which "the rot will spread"?

There is only one sensible answer to this question. The rot that concerns planners is the threat of successful social and economic development outside the framework of U.S. control, development of a sort that may be meaningful to poor and oppressed people elsewhere. The "virus" that may spread contagion is the "demonstration effect," which may indeed cause "the rot to spread" as others seek to emulate successes that they observe. It is "the threat of a good example."

In the 1950s, U.S. planners were deeply concerned over the possibility of successful social and economic development in North Vietnam and China, and in South Vietnam under the NLF if the "internal aggression" should succeed. This might lead to efforts to emulate their achievements elsewhere, so that Southeast Asia would no longer "fulfill its function" as a dependency of Japan and the West, serving their needs rather than its own. It was feared that ultimately Japan, an industrial power dependent on foreign markets and resources, would "accommodate" to a new emerging system in Asia, becoming the industrial heartland of a region to which the U.S. would not have privileged access. The U.S. had fought World War II in the Pacific to prevent Japan from creating a "co-prosperity sphere" of this sort, and was not inclined to lose World War II in the early postwar period. U.S. policymakers were therefore committed to ensure that the rot would not spread. In this context, Vietnam attained a significance far beyond its own meager importance in the world system.

In the 1950s, U.S. planners recommended that measures should be taken to impede economic development in China and North Vietnam, a proposal that is remarkable in its cruelty. They fought a vicious war to ensure that no successes in Indochina would "infect the region"—a war that succeeded in its major aims, a matter to which I will return.

Similarly, Kissinger was concerned that Allende's democratic socialism might send the "wrong message" to voters in European democracies. Therefore it was necessary to prevent the "virus" from "spreading contagion," in a manner that is well-known. The same was true of the efforts of Arévalo and Arbenz to establish independent democratic capitalism geared to the needs of the domestic population in Guatemala. Similarly, the CIA warned in 1964 that Cuba "is being watched closely by other nations in the hemisphere and any appearance of success there would have an extensive impact on the statist trend elsewhere in the area," endangering the Fifth Freedom. It was therefore necessary to persist in the terrorist war launched by Kennedy against Cuba after the failure of the Bay of Pigs invasion, while maintaining a hostile posture designed to ensure that Cuba would remain dependent on the USSR and would not achieve "an appearance of success."

Much the same has been true in many other cases, including Nicaragua today. The early successes of the Sandinistas quite rightly caused fear, indeed virtual hysteria among U.S. elites, as we see from the fact that the government can declare a "national emergency" in the face of this grave threat to the existence of the United States without evoking ridicule, indeed, with the expressed support of respectable opinion. If peasants starving to death in Honduras can look across the borders and see health clinics, land reform, literacy programs, improvement in subsistence agriculture and the like in a country no better endowed than their own, the rot may spread; and it may spread still farther, perhaps even to the United States, where the many people suffering from malnutrition or the homeless in the streets in the world's richest country may begin to ask some questions. It is necessary to destroy the rotten apple before the rot spreads through the barrel. The same fears were evoked by the growth of popular organizations in El Salvador in the 1970s, which threatened to lead to meaningful democracy in which resources would be directed to domestic needs, an intolerable attack on the Fifth Freedom. There are numerous other cases.

That planners understand these matters is evident not only from the consistent invocation of the rotten apple theory and the regular resort to violence and other measures to prevent the rot from spreading, but also from the deceitful manner in which state propaganda is presented. The most recent State Department effort to prove Nicaraguan aggressiveness, published in September 1985 in obvious response to the World Court proceedings after the U.S. refusal to accept lawful means to settle the Central American conflicts it had created, is entitled *Revolution Beyond Our Borders*. The title is allegedly drawn from a speech by Tomás Borge, and the cover features a mistranslation of a passage from this 1981 speech. In the original, Borge says that "this revolution transcends national boundaries," making it clear that he means ideological transcendence and adding: "this does not mean we export our revolution. It is enough—and we couldn't do otherwise—for us to export our example . . . we know that it is the people themselves of these countries who must make their revolutions." This is the statement that was deformed and then exploited by the U.S. disinformation system—including the media, as we shall see—as proof that Nicaragua actually boasts of its planned "aggression."

Here we see a clear example of the switch between the two variants of the domino theory: the real concern of privileged elites over the demonstration effect of successful development becomes transmuted, for the public, into a pretended concern that the U.S. will once again be at the mercy of yellow dwarves with pocket knives, who will conquer everything in their path, finally stealing all we have, while the "bound and throttled giant" is unable to prevent this aggression. The deceit is *so* transparent and so contrived that it is surely an instance of conscious manipulation by unscrupulous propagandists—who are protected from exposure in the mainstream media, a fact from which we can draw further consequences.

I should add that deception of this kind is quite common, including what is called "scholarship." Elsewhere, I have documented the fact that during the Vietnam years, the government and respected American commentators grossly misrepresented the contents of "captured documents" in exactly the same way, continuing to do so even after the deception was exposed, secure in the knowledge that the exposure, outside of the mainstream, would remain essentially irrelevant among the educated classes whom they address (University of Massachusetts historian Guenter Lewy, in the latter case, in a highly regarded work of "scholarship" justifying the U.S. "defense" of South Vietnam).

In the case of Nicaragua, U.S. officials state openly that while they doubt that the contras can depose the present government, "they are content to see the contras debilitate the Sandinistas by forcing them to divert scarce resources toward the war and away from social programs" *(Boston Globe* correspondent Julia Preston, citing "Administration officials"). The suffering and economic chaos that result from the attacks by the U.S. proxy armies are then exploited, in the usual manner, to justify the aggression in terms of "the failures of the revolution," with the mass media regularly parroting the government line, again as usual. The ultimate display of moral cowardice is the allegation that the Sandinistas actually welcome the contra attacks, which provide them with an excuse to conceal their failures and repression, a common refrain of liberal critics of the Reagan Administration.

It is interesting that the cynical and horrifying statements of the Administration officials cited by Julia Preston, and others like them, are blandly reported, evoking no comment, quickly forgotten. In cultivated Western circles, it is considered the prerogative of the United States to use violence to prevent reform measures that might benefit poor and deprived people, so that the statement of such an intent arouses no special interest or concern. The U.S. will permit no constructive programs in its own domains, so it must ensure that they are destroyed elsewhere, to undermine "the threat of a good example."

The latter phrase is used as the title of a pamphlet on Nicaragua by the charitable development agency Oxfam, which observes that "from Oxfam's experience of working in seventy-six developing countries, Nicaragua was to prove exceptional in the strength of that Government's commitment. . .to improving the condition of the people and encouraging their active participation in the development process," providing numerous examples. The title of the pamphlet is well-chosen. It is precisely these features of the Sandinista revolution that sent chills up the spines of U.S. planners, and privileged elites elsewhere as well. Their pretended concern over repression in Nicaragua, and various real or alleged Sandinista crimes, cannot be taken seriously by any sane person; even if the harshest charges with a shred of credibility are accepted, the Sandinista leadership is positively saintly in comparison with the gangsters that the U.S. has supported throughout Central America and beyond, not to speak of Washington itself. The real crime of the Sandinistas is the one identified by the Oxfam report and affirmed by many others, including the international lending institutions. The crime is to have posed the threat of a good example, which may "infect" the region, and even beyond.

The rotten apple theory explains another wise curious feature of U.S. foreign policy: the profound concern evoked by developments in the tiniest and most marginal countries, such as Laos or Grenada, for example. In the 1960s, northern Laos was subjected to the heaviest bombing in history (soon to be exceeded in Cambodia), what is called a "secret bombing"; this is another technical term, referring to bombing that was well-known to the media but suppressed in service to the state, and later used as evidence of government deceit when it became necessary to remove a political leader who had made the unconscionable error of attacking powerful domestic enemies, people quite capable of defending themselves (the Watergate farce, to which I will return in lecture 5). As the U.S. Administration conceded in Congressional hearings, the bombing was unrelated to the war in Vietnam. Rather, it was directed against the Pathet Lao guerrillas, who were attempting to carry out mild social reforms and to introduce a sense of national identity in the scattered villages of northern Laos, where few people even knew they were in Laos. Or consider Grenada, a tiny speck in the Caribbean of no interest to the United States, where the Maurice Bishop government at once elicited U.S. hostility and rage, including economic measures and threatening military maneuvers and finally, after the regime cracked, outright invasion.

Why should such tiny and marginal countries evoke such concern, indeed near hysteria, among U.S. planners? Surely their resources are of no significance. And while indeed leading U.S. military and political figures solemnly discussed the military threat posed by Grenada, one must assume that these ravings—for that is what they are—were simply a cover for something else. An explanation for this superficially quite irrational behavior is provided by the rotten apple theory, in its internal rather than public form; in these terms, the hysteria makes perfect sense. If a tiny and impoverished country with minuscule resources can begin to do something for its own population, others may ask: "Why not us?" The weaker and more insignificant a country, the more limited its means and resources, the greater is the threat of a good example. The rot may spread, threatening regions of real concern to the rulers of much of the world.

The rotten apple theory, as noted, follows from the basic principle of policy: the defense of the Fifth Freedom. It quite naturally has two variants: the public variant designed to frighten the population at large, and the internal variant that consistently guides planning. This typical duality is a consequence of the second principle of policy: the need to ensure public ignorance and conformity. The public plainly cannot be informed of the true motives of policy, and the educated classes have the task, which they perform with diligence and success, of protecting the general public from any understanding of such critical matters. It should be noted that they also protect themselves from any dangerous understanding of reality, as the political leadership also does to an extent, at least the less intelligent among them. In public as in personal life, it is extremely easy to deceive oneself about the motives for one's actions, placing a favorable construction on actions taken for quite different ends. Hitler may well have believed that he was defending Germany from the "aggression" of the Poles and excising the "cancer" of the Jews, and George Shultz may believe that he is defending the United States from the "aggression" of Grenada and excising the Sandinista "cancer," as he and other Administration officials regularly declaim. We have no difficulty in detecting the real motives and plans in the first case, though sophisticated German intellectuals pretended—to themselves and others—to be unable to do so during the Hitler years. And those who can extricate themselves from the Western doctrinal system should have no greater difficulty in detecting the real motives in the second case, and numerous others like it.

I might mention again that there is little that is new in the various formulations of the rotten apple theory. In the early 19th century, conservative European statesmen (Metternich, the Czar and his diplomats) spoke in similar terms of the "pernicious doctrines of republicanism and popular self-rule," "evil doctrines and pernicious examples" that might spread from the United States "over the whole of America" and even to Europe, undermining the conservative moral and political order that was the foundation of civilization. It is not surprising that the contemporary inheritors of the role of the Czar and Metternich should think along similar lines, even using similar rhetoric, and with similar moralistic pretensions, which they take quite seriously, as do the conformist intellectuals quite generally in the media, journals of opinion, and respectable scholarship.

So far, I have discussed several related elements of the international system that emerged from the wreckage of World War II, still largely focusing on the dominant U.S. role: some of the costs of great power intervention, primarily Western, in the Third World; the problem of incorporating Western and Southern Europe within the Grand Area while Eastern Europe was subordinated to Soviet power; the postwar campaign to destroy the anti-fascist resistance; the rotten apple theory and its applications. Let us turn now to a few remarks on what is commonly regarded as the central feature of the modern global system: the superpower rivalry, the Cold War.

In the early postwar period, the U.S. hoped to incorporate the Soviet Union within the Grand Area: the "roll-back strategy" of NSC-68 was motivated by that goal. It soon became evident that this was hopeless, and the superpowers settled into an uneasy form of coexistence that we call the Cold War. The real meaning of the Cold War is elucidated by a look at its typical events: Soviet tanks in East Berlin in 1953, in Budapest in 1956, in Prague in 1968, the invasion of Afghanistan; U.S. intervention in Greece, Iran, Guatemala, Indochina, Cuba, the Dominican Republic, Chile, El Salvador and Nicaragua, and a host of other examples, including U.S.-backed aggression by client states, as in East Timor and Lebanon, among other instances. In each case, when one of the superpowers resorts to subversion or aggression, the act is presented to the domestic population and the allies as "self-defense," defense against the superpower enemy or its agents. In fact, the actions are taken to ensure control over a certain sphere of influence; for the U.S., much of the world.

The actual events of the Cold War illustrate the fact that the Cold War is in effect a system of joint global management, a system with a certain functional utility for the superpowers, one reason why it persists. Intervention and subversion are conducted in the interest of elite groups, what is called in political theology "the national interest," meaning the special interest of groups with sufficient domestic power to shape affairs of state. But, these exercises of state violence are often quite costly to the general population in both material and moral terms—and the latter should not be discounted, as is often done in a display of pretended sophistication that is hardly more than an expression of self-righteous elite contempt for ordinary people, contempt that is as unwarranted as it is uninformed. Domestic policies too are conducted in the interest of dominant elites, but are often quite costly for the general population: militarization of the society, for example. To mobilize the population and recalcitrant allies in support of costly domestic programs and foreign adventures, it is necessary to appeal to the fear of some Great Satan, to adopt the Ayatollah Khomeini's useful contribution to political rhetoric. The Cold War confrontation provides a useful means. Of course, it is necessary to avoid direct confrontation with the Great Satan himself, this being far too dangerous. It is preferable to confront weak and defenseless powers designated as proxies of the Great Satan. The Reagan Administration has regularly used Libya for this purpose, arranging regular confrontations timed to domestic needs, for example, the need to gain support for the Rapid Deployment Force or for contra aid. The system is a hazardous one, and may sooner or later break down, leading to a terminal global war, something that has come close to happening more than once and will again. But this is the kind of long-term consideration that does not enter into planning. I will return to closer consideration of this matter in the fourth lecture.

This all-too-brief review of the postwar global system is partial and hence somewhat misleading; thus, I have said nothing about U.S. policies in the Middle East, which are crucial for an understanding of the current world, or about developing conflicts among the industrial capitalist states, among other topics. Before turning to Central America, in the next lecture, I will conclude this general review with a few remarks on the U.S. engagement in Indochina, a major event of modern history and one from which we can learn a great deal about U.S. policy planning, with significant implications for Central America today. In this case, we have an extremely rich documentary record, which is very revealing although (or perhaps more accurately: therefore) generally ignored in the extensive public discussion on the topic.

By 1948, the U.S. recognized that the Viet Minh led by Ho Chi Minh was in effect the Vietnamese nationalist movement and that it would be difficult to achieve any solution excluding it. Nonetheless, the U.S. committed itself to exactly that goal, supporting the French effort to reconquer their former colony. The central reasons for this decision I have already discussed: they follow from the rotten apple theory and the concern that Southeast Asia "fulfill its function" in the U.S.-dominated global order.

Naturally, matters could not be presented in these terms. Once the U.S. had committed itself to supporting the French attack, it became a necessary truth that France was defending Indochina from the "internal aggression" of the Viet Minh, and that Ho was simply a puppet of Moscow (or China; either would do). U.S. Intelligence was assigned the task of demonstrating this necessary truth, and made noble efforts to do so. It failed. Intelligence reported that it was able to find evidence of "Kremlin-directed conspiracy . . . in virtually all countries except Vietnam." The task, then, was to use this discovery to establish the required conclusion, a step that was simple enough: "it may be assumed," U.S. officials concluded, "that Moscow feels that Ho and his lieutenants have had sufficient training and experience and are sufficiently loyal to be trusted to determine their day-to-day policy without supervision." Thus the lack of contact between Ho and his masters in the Kremlin establishes that he is a loyal slave of Moscow, as required.

One of the most startling revelations in the *Pentagon Papers* is that in a review of U.S. intelligence covering 25 years, the Pentagon analysts were able to discover only one staff paper that even raised the question whether Hanoi was pursuing its own interests instead of just acting as an agent of the "Kremlin-directed conspiracy." Even U.S. intelligence, which is paid to discover the facts and not to rave about Soviet plans to conquer the world, was unable to escape the grips of the propaganda system, a most revealing fact. Whatever one thinks of Ho Chi Minh and his associates, the fact that they were pursuing Vietnamese national interests as they perceived them rather than merely following Soviet orders is utterly transparent and not in doubt among sane people, but it was beyond the comprehension of U.S. intelligence, an intriguing reflection of the prevailing cultural climate.

In this record we see dramatically revealed one of the central features of U.S. foreign policy. A popular movement or a state does not become an enemy because it is controlled by Moscow; rather, given that it is an enemy (for other reasons) and therefore must be undermined and destroyed, it must be that it is controlled by Moscow, whatever the facts, so that the U.S. attack against it is just and necessary. The "other reasons" are those already discussed. The U.S. may indeed succeed in driving the enemy into the hands of the Russians by its hostile actions, a most welcome result, or if it fails, it will pretend that this is the case, trusting the media to go along, as in the case of Guatemala in 1954, for example. Naturally, none of this can be expressed within the doctrinal system, and indeed it is not.

From 1950 to 1954 the U.S. sought to impose French rule over Indochina, but failed. In 1954, France withdrew, and the Geneva Agreements established a basis for peace. The United States devoted itself at once to undermining them, and succeeded. Thanks to U.S. subversion and its dominance of the international system, the provisional demarcation line at the 17th parallel became an "international boundary"—though the U.S.-imposed client regime in the South never accepted it, regarding itself as the government of all Vietnam. Its official name, throughout, was the Government of Vietnam (GVN), and this pretension was reiterated in an unamendable article of its Constitution, produced under U.S. auspices.

In the South, the U.S. imposed a terrorist regime on the familiar Latin American model. From 1954 to 1960, this client state had massacred perhaps some 75,000 people. Its terrorism and repression evoked renewed resistance—naturally called "Communist aggression," "internal aggression" in Adlai Stevenson 's phrase—at which point the regime virtually collapsed and the U.S. was compelled to intervene directly. In 1962, the U.S. began extensive bombing and defoliation of South Vietnam as part of an effort to drive several million people into concentration camps where they would be surrounded by barbed wire and "protected" from the South Vietnamese guerrillas (the NLF; in U.S. terminology, "Viet Cong") whom they were willingly supporting, as the U.S. conceded. For the next few years, the U.S. desperately sought to block a political settlement, including the neutralization of South Vietnam, Laos and Cambodia proposed by the NLF. Unable to find suitable clients in the South, the U.S. replaced government after government and finally, in 1964, decided to escalate the attack against South Vietnam with a direct land invasion accompanied by bombing of North Vietnam, a program initiated in early 1965. Throughout all of this period, no North Vietnamese regulars were detected in South Vietnam, though they had every right to be there after the U.S. subversion of the Geneva Agreements and the terror launched in the South. By April 1965, when the U.S. invaded South Vietnam outright, deaths there probably amounted to close to 200,000. While it was the bombing of North Vietnam that attracted international attention, the main U.S. attack, including bombing, was always directed against South Vietnam. Once again, U.S. hegemony in the international system is reflected by the fact that there is no such event in recorded history as the U.S. attack against South Vietnam (rather sanitized history records only a U.S. "defense" of South Vietnam, which was unwise, the official doves later maintained), and the attack was never recognized as such nor condemned by the United Nations.

These facts merit serious consideration for those interested in Western intellectual culture and the dominance of U.S. power in the global system. The U.S. attack against South Vietnam from 1962, escalated and expanded in scope in 1965, plainly took place, just as much as the Soviet invasion of Afghanistan did in 1979; furthermore, South Vietnam was the main target of the U.S. attack. In both cases, the aggressors claimed to have been "invited in" by a legal government that they were defending against "bandits" and "terrorists" supported from abroad. Soviet claims in this regard, on their border, are no less credible than those of the U.S. for its aggression 10,000 miles away; that is, the credibility is zero in both cases. Nevertheless, the U.S., the West, and indeed most of the world, do not recognize the existence of such an event as the U.S. attack against South Vietnam, though few are unable to perceive that the USSR invaded Afghanistan, and indeed this invasion is regularly condemned not only by Western governments but also by the United Nations. Even in peace movement circles, as activists will recall, it was virtually impossible to discuss U.S. operations in South Vietnam honestly: as aggression against the South under the cover of a farcical government established (and regularly replaced, until willing elements could be created) to serve to legitimate the aggression. Neither the media, nor mainstream scholarship, record any such event as the U.S. aggression against South Vietnam. Furthermore, this denial of plain reality extends over most of the world. These are remarkable and highly instructive facts. It is also worthy of note that it is now becoming somewhat easier to speak of these events honestly in public, though rarely in educated circles, a mark of the increased sophistication and understanding of much of the public during the years when it is falsely alleged that a "conservative revival" has taken place, a matter to which I will return in the last lecture.

From 1965 the U.S. expanded its war against South Vietnam, sending an invading army that reached over half a million men by 1968. It also accelerated the attack against the northern half of the artificially divided country, began the murderous bombing of Laos, and extended its violations of Cambodian neutrality, finally initiating another "secret bombing" in 1969 and invading Cambodia outright in 1970 after a U.S.-backed military coup. This was followed by civil war and bombardment at an incredible scale, with hundreds of thousands killed and the country virtually destroyed.

Meanwhile, a popular movement against the Indochina wars began to develop at home, reaching significant proportions by 1967. The major achievement of the peace movement was to prevent the government from carrying out a full-scale national mobilization. It was forced to fight a "guns-and-butter war," with deficit financing, harming the U.S. economy and laying the basis for the crisis of following years. As a result, U.S. power declined relative to its real rivals, Europe and Japan, the latter now becoming a serious competitor thanks to the costs of the Vietnam war, harmful to the United States but highly beneficial to Japan, which enriched itself by its participation in the destruction of Indochina, as did Canada and other U.S. allies. In January 1968, the Tet offensive caused virtual panic in Washington, and led American business elites to conclude that the investment should be liquidated. A corporate-based delegation of "wise men" was dispatched to Washington to inform Lyndon Johnson that he was finished, and that the government must turn to "Vietnamization," that is, withdrawal of U.S. troops and a more capital-intensive war.

The war continued for seven more years, reaching its peak of savagery in South Vietnam with the 1969-1970 Post-Tet "accelerated pacification campaign," a mass murder operation to which the My Lai massacre was one minor footnote, trivial in context.

In January 1973, the U.S. was compelled to sign the Peace Treaty it had rejected the preceding November. What happened next was a virtual replay of 1954, which should be observed carefully by those who enter into negotiations involving the United States. On the day of the signing of the Paris Treaty, Washington announced, quite publicly, that it would reject every major element of the treaty that it signed. The central article of the Paris accords stated that there are two parallel and equivalent "parties" in South Vietnam (the U.S.-backed GVN and the PRG, formerly the NLF); these two parties were to come to an agreement without the interference of any foreign power (meaning: the U.S.), and were then to move towards settlement and integration with the northern half of the country, again without U.S. interference. Washington signed the agreement, but announced that in violation of it, the U.S. would continue to support the GVN as the "sole legitimate government in South Vietnam," "its constitutional structure and leadership intact and unchanged." This "constitutional structure" outlawed the second of the two parallel and equivalent parties in the South, and explicitly nullified the articles of the treaty that laid the basis for reconciliation and peaceful settlement. Similarly, every other major element of the treaty would be violated, the U.S. announced.

The mass media, in an illuminating exercise of servility to the state, adopted the Washington version of the Paris accords as the operative one, thus guaranteeing that as the U.S. continued to violate the treaty, the PRG and North Vietnam would appear to be in violation of it and could then be condemned as unconscionable aggressors. That is precisely what happened, exactly as was predicted at the time by the tiny group of dissidents in the U.S. among the articulate intelligentsia, who were carefully excluded from any forum where they might reach a substantial audience. The U.S.-GVN moved at once to extend their control over South Vietnam by force, in violation of the scrap of paper they had signed in Paris. When the inevitable PRG-North Vietnam reaction took place, it was bitterly condemned as yet another example of unprovoked "Communist aggression," and so official doctrine now records. The true story is missing from sanitized history, though one can find the facts in the marginalized dissident literature, which is easily ignored.

The lessons of 1954 and 1973 are very clear, and the victims of U.S. violence will ignore them at their peril.

Though the U.S. government tactic succeeded brilliantly in the United States and the West in general, it failed in Vietnam.

Despite enormous U.S. military support, the GVN collapsed. By April 1975, the U.S. client regimes had been defeated. Most of Indochina, or what was left of it, was under effective North Vietnamese control since apart from Cambodia, the resistance movements—particularly, the NLF in South Vietnam—had been unable to survive the savage U.S. assault, again, exactly as had been predicted years earlier by marginalized dissidents. This predictable (and predicted) consequence of U.S. aggression was, of course, at once used in justification of the aggression that created these conditions, exactly as one would expect of a properly disciplined intellectual community.

Note that all of this took place at the moment when the media had reached their peak of dissidence, priding themselves on their "independence" from the state with the Watergate exposures and the controversy over Vietnam. It is worthy of note that the two examples regularly adduced as proof of the courage and independence of the media—Vietnam and Watergate—in fact provide dramatic evidence of their subordination to state power, along with the educated classes generally.

In the reconstruction of history that has since become approved doctrine, the media are depicted as having adopted an "adversarial stance" with regard to the state during this period, perhaps so much so as to undermine democratic institutions. This is alleged not only by the rightwing, but also by liberal opinion. The charge is made, for example, in an important study called *The Crisis of Democracy* published by the Trilateral Commission, an elite group of generally liberal persuasion (the group that supported Jimmy Carter and filled virtually every top executive position during his Administration), organized by David Rockefeller in 1973 with representatives from the three centers of industrial capitalist democracy: the U.S., Europe and Japan. The "crisis of democracy" that they deplore arose during the 1960s, when normally passive and apathetic elements of the population began to enter the political arena, threatening what is called "democracy" in the West: the unchallenged rule by privileged elites. The alleged "adversarial stance" of the media towards the state was one of the most dangerous features of this "crisis of democracy," the Commission study maintains, a danger that must be overcome. The true nature of this "media dissidence" is exhibited by the remarkable story of the Paris Peace Treaty along with much else, as one can learn, once again, from the marginalized dissident literature, though the "crisis of democracy" was real enough among the general population, and has not yet been overcome, despite dedicated efforts in the post-Vietnam years.

It is commonly held that the U.S. lost the war and that North Vietnam was victorious. This is taken for granted as an unquestionable truth in mainstream U.S. and European opinion, as well as in the U.S. peace movement and the left in Europe. The conclusion, however, is incorrect, and it is important to understand why. The U.S. government won a partial victory in Indochina, though it suffered a major defeat at home, where the domestic effects of the war were very significant, accelerating the growth of popular movements that entirely changed the cultural climate over a large range and for a time threatened elite dominance of the political system, bringing about "the crisis of democracy." Much of the population—though not educated elites, with rare exceptions—was afflicted with a dread disease called "the Vietnam syndrome," which persists until today and I hope is incurable: namely, opposition to aggression and massacre and a sense of solidarity and sympathy with the victims. I will turn to this matter, which is of great importance, in the last lecture. Much of the political history of the 1970s has been an elite counterattack to overcome the "crisis of democracy" and the "Vietnam syndrome."

But what about Indochina itself? Here, the United States had a maximum objective and a minimum objective. The maxi-

mum objective was to turn Vietnam into another earthly para-
dise such as Chile or Guatemala or the Philippines. The minimum objective was to prevent the rot from spreading, possibly
with major consequences extending as far as Japan, as I discussed earlier. The U.S. failed to achieve its maximal objective:
Vietnam has not been incorporated into the U.S. global system.
But despite much inflated rhetoric by Eisenhower and others
about the rubber, tin and rice of Indochina, and later talk about
oil, it was never of much importance to extend the Fifth Freedom to Indochina itself. The major concern was to excise the
"cancer," in George Shultz's current phrase, to kill the "virus"
and prevent it from "infecting" regions beyond. This objective
was attained. Indochina was largely destroyed, and crucially, the
dangerous popular movement in South Vietnam was virtually
eradicated by U.S. terror. Indochina will be lucky to survive, and
postwar U.S. policy has been designed to maximize suffering
and repression there—including refusal of promised reparations,
barriers to aid and trade, support for Pol Pot, and similar measures familiar enough here in Managua. The cruelty of these postwar measures reveals the significance assigned to ensuring that
there will be no recovery from the devastation of the U.S. assault. To mention a few examples, the U.S. government attempted to prevent India from sending 100 buffalos (for an
underdeveloped peasant society, that means fertilizer, the equivalent of tractors, etc.) to replenish the herds destroyed by U.S.
aggression, and even tried to prevent shipment of pencils to
Cambodia after Vietnam had overthrown the murderous Democratic Kampuchea government, a government that the U.S.
now supports because of its "continuity" with the Pol Pot
regime, the State Department has explained. It is of critical importance to ensure that there will be no recovery for a long, long
rime to come, and that the ruined lands will be firmly in the Soviet bloc to justify further hostile actions.

Meanwhile the U.S. strengthened what was called "the second line of defense." The attack on the "virus" was two-pronged: it was necessary to destroy it at the source, and to "inoculate" the region to prevent the "infection" from spreading "contagion" beyond. The U.S. established and supported murderous and repressive regimes in Indonesia in 1965, in the Philippines in 1972, in Thailand in the 1970s, to ensure that "the second line of defense" would not be breached. As I mentioned earlier, the 1965 Suharto military coup in Indonesia with its murderous consequences—the slaughter of hundreds of thousands of landless peasants—was lauded in the West, by liberal opinion as well, and was offered as justification for the "defense" of South Vietnam, which provided a "shield" behind which the Indonesian generals were encouraged to purge their society of the mass-based Communist Party and open it up to Western plunder, impeded only by the rapacity of the generals and their cohorts.

There is no "threat of a good example" in Indochina, and surrounding regions, the ones that were really important, are firmly incorporated within the Grand Area. The current problems have more to do with rivalries within the First World of industrial capitalism than with the threat of "infection" that might lead to independent development geared to domestic needs. All of this counts as a substantial success for the U.S. crusade in Indochina, a fact of which business circles, at least, have long been well aware.

The doctrinal system regards the war as a U.S. defeat: for those of unlimited ambition, a failure to achieve maximal aims is always a tragedy, and it is true, and important, that elite groups suffered a defeat at home, with the eruption of the "crisis of democracy" and the growth of the "Vietnam syndrome." The fact that others accept this conclusion may in part be a result of the remarkable hegemony of the U.S. propaganda system, and in part a reflection of the understandable desire to record a "victory" for popular protest, which was often undertaken at quite considerable personal cost, particularly among the young, who spearheaded the anti-war movement. But there should be no illusions about what actually happened. The popular movements did achieve a great deal. Indochina at least survives; the U.S. did not resort to nuclear weapons as it might well have done had the population remained docile and quiescent, as it was during the terror of the U.S.-imposed regime in the South, or when Kennedy launched the direct U.S. attack against the South in 1962. But the "lesson of Vietnam," which was taught with extreme brutality and sadism, is that those who try to defend their independence from the Global Enforcer may pay a fearful cost. Many others have been subjected to similar lessons, in Central America as well.

I will turn to this topic in the next lecture.

Lecture 2: Discussion March 2, 1986

QUESTION: We feel that through what you say and write you are our friend but at the same time you talk about North American imperialism and Russian imperialism in the same breath. I ask you how you can use the same arguments as reactionaries such as Octavio Paz, Vargas Llosa, etc.

ANSWER: I have been accused of everything and that therefore includes being a reactionary. From my personal experience there are two countries in which my political writings can basically not appear. One is the U.S. within the mainstream with very rare exceptions. The other is the USSR. I would personally not want to be associated with Vargas Llosa, Octavio Paz, and the rest. I think what we ought to do is to try to understand the truth about the world. And the truth about the world is usually quite unpleasant.

One of the truths about the world is that there are two superpowers, one a huge power which happens to have its boot on your neck, another, a smaller power which happens to have its boot on other people's necks. In fact these two superpowers have a form of tacit cooperation in controlling much of the world.

My own concern is primarily the terror and violence carried out by my own state, for two reasons. For one thing, because it happens to be the larger component of international violence. But also for a much more important reason than that; namely, I can do something about it. So even if the U.S. was responsible for 2 percent of the violence in the world instead of the majority of it, it would be that 2 percent I would be primarily responsible for. And that is a simple ethical judgment. That is, the ethical value of one's actions depends on their anticipated and predictable consequences. It is very easy to denounce the atrocities of someone else. That has about as much ethical value as denouncing atrocities that took place in the 18th century.

The point is that the useful and significant political actions
are those that have consequences for human beings. And those
are overwhelmingly the actions which you have some way of in-
fluencing and controlling, which means for me, American actions. But I am also involved in protesting Soviet imperialism,
and also explaining its roots in Soviet society. And I think that
anyone in the Third World would be making a grave error if they
succumbed to illusions about these matters.

QUESTION: (Blank) . . . Was Stalin hostile to Mao?

ANSWER: In fact Stalin was supporting Chiang Kai-Shek
against the Chinese revolution. The subsequent and rather brief
alliance was in part the result of U.S. policies. The U.S. had to
choose between two policies after 1949. One policy was to adopt
a militant and aggressive posture towards China and try to drive
it into the hands of the Soviet Union—that was the policy of the
hawks. The proposal of the doves was to try to enter into trade
and commercial relations with China and to gradually absorb it
into the American sphere. The doves argued that American
power was so enormous and China so weak that if we did enter
into peaceful relations with it we could reverse the Chinese revolution and bring China within the U.S. system. Each of the positions was represented by a very substantial part of American
business and in fact the debate went on among business circles
through the early part of the 1950s.

Notice that they both had the same goals. The goal was to
ensure that China would be reincorporated within the Grand
Area. They differed on the measures that should be used to
achieve this end. Now, the hawks won the debate and until 1970
the U.S. engaged in a very hostile policy towards China and tried
very hard to ensure that China would be subordinated to the Soviet Union. By 1960 it was completely obvious that China and

Russia were very hostile and this hostility developed through the l 960s until finally they almost went to war. Throughout that period American planners pretended it was not happening; some of them claimed that it was simply a pretense to fool the U.S. The point is, it was necessary for China to be subordinated to Russia in order to justify our hostile policies towards China and therefore the perfectly obvious facts did not matter at all.

Now, by 1970, U.S. planners began to realize that this policy was not working and then Nixon and Kissinger shifted to the opposite policy, namely to try to incorporate China within the American system by diplomacy, trade, commercial relations, and so on, and to use China in the American confrontation with the USSR. And in fact that policy is being continued until today; so, for example, China supports Pol Pot who attacks Cambodia from bases in Thailand and this is part of the American alliance designed to make Cambodia and Vietnam suffer as much as possible.

QUESTION: How is it possible that the intelligent elites of the U.S. are not the people in sympathy with the protest movements, considering that the common masses in the U.S. are victims of the Mass Media propaganda and disinformation in television, etc.? How can you explain this fact?

ANSWER: We are mostly intellectuals, and intellectuals like to consider themselves as being very smart and enlightened. And of course intellectuals are the people who write history and do sociology. So the picture of the world that intellectuals present is that the stupid masses are ignorant and understand nothing while the intellectuals are fine, intelligent, ethical, and far-sighted people. Well, people who are sophisticated enough to apply class analysis and trace actions to their economic and other roots should apply the same kind of analysis to intellectuals and their interests. So, we have to ask whether, as a matter of fact, intellectuals are indeed enlightened, free, ethical, and so on, while the mass of the people are terrible and ignorant and understand nothing.

I think that the lesson of history is that this is very often not the case. In the last century in particular, a period in which the intelligentsia have developed as a more or less identifiable category in modern societies, they have tended to see themselves as managers, either managers of industry, managers of the state or ideological managers. That has been the general tendency among the intelligentsia, that is the interest that they hope to satisfy. And that, incidentally, is true in Western capitalist societies, in the so-called "socialist" societies (which are not socialist, in my opinion), and in the Third World. We have to ask what kind of an image of the world these intellectuals have created and why.

Well, they have created an image of a stupid mass who must be led by clever intellectuals. In fact, what we often find is that the intellectuals, the educated classes, are the most indoctrinated, most ignorant, most stupid part of the population, and there are very good reasons for that. Basically two reasons. First of all, as the literate part of the population, they are subjected to the mass of propaganda. There is a second, more important and more subtle reason. Namely, they are the ideological managers. Therefore, they must internalize the propaganda and believe it. And part of the propaganda they have developed is that they are the natural leaders of the masses. Now sometimes that is true but often it is not.

The U.S. is a society which is very heavily polled. The reason is that business wants to better understand what the popular mood is, so we have a great deal of information about popular attitudes divided by sectors of the population and so on. Every year the Gallup Poll, a major poll, asks people: Do you think the Vietnam war was a "mistake" or do you think it was "fundamentally wrong and immoral"? Among the general population, over 70 percent say that it was "fundamentally wrong and immoral."

Among the groups that they call "opinion leaders," which include people like clergymen, it is about 40 percent who think that the war was "fundamentally wrong and immoral." Among the intellectual elite, other studies show that the overwhelming majority regarded it as a mistake only, always, even at the height of the war. That is not unusual.

We may be misled about this because it was often intellectuals who were prominent in opposition to the war. They were the people who were making the speeches and writing the articles, but in fact, it was a tiny fraction of the intellectuals, and as in the case of most popular movements, the effective grassroots activists are unknown to the general public, or to history.

I think this is rather generally the case, and it is a fact with a great many implications for social policy and its many domains.

QUESTION: Towards the end of your presentation here the strategic hamlets in Vietnam were mentioned, although you did not use that particular term. I also have had documentation and have read recently about the resettlement for defense in the highlands of Peru which has really served the same purpose, and last month had the interesting experience of being in a *pueblo de desarrollo* (or model village) in the north of Guatemala which serves the same purpose basically, to absorb the landless population to remove support from the guerrillas and to remove possible individuals who might be involved in the guerrilla movement. I would like to know if you have any information on the planning for this kind of strategy; where it was developed; has it been carried out for the same purpose in other parts of the world?

ANSWER: This policy in one form or another goes quite far back in history. For example, the British used something like it in the Boer war in South Africa at the turn of the century. The modern version is more sophisticated. It was developed extensively by

the British in Malaya in the 1950s in putting down a peasant insurgency there. And the idea was carried over, in fact using the
same British advisers, to Vietnam in the 1960s.

I did not use the official term "Strategic Hamlets" but rather
the term "concentration camps," which I think is more appropriate
in Vietnam. The attempt was made to drive about 7 million people
into camps where they would be surrounded by barbed wire and
the security forces would be able to go and pick out the dangerous
people and kill them and the population would be controlled by
force. Well, it did not work in Vietnam. The people who planned
it complained that they were never able to weed out the guerrillas.
The counterinsurgency experts of the Kennedy Administration—
Roger Hilsman, for example—said that the peasants in the concentration camps could not have a "free choice" because the Viet
Cong cadres had not all been killed. It's a lot like the "free elections" in El Salvador. First you murder the opposition. Then you
have a free election. This is the same idea.

The idea has been developed and refined exactly as you say.
One of the major operations is in Guatemala, where there were
advisers from many countries; apparently from Argentina under
the Nazi generals, and from Israel, and from elsewhere. One part
of the counterinsurgency campaign was just massacre, which was
very large, and the other was placing the population in concentration camps called "model villages." In fact, I could list many
other examples where the same thing is done.

Let me just mention one more, in another part of the world.
I mentioned the war in Timor. This was an Indonesian invasion,
supported by the U.S. The victim was another potential rotten
apple, a tiny, poor country which had won its independence
when the Portuguese empire collapsed and began to carry out
mild social reforms and national development. It was subjected
at once to a very brutal Indonesian attack supported and armed
by the U.S. About one-quarter of the population was murdered

and most of the rest have been put in resettlement camps, where they can be controlled. This is a very natural policy for an aggressor state, and of course they learn to do it better every time. We can be sure that it's going to be a pattern which will be repeated in the future.

LECTURE 3

Our Little Region Over Here

Your primary interest of course is Central America today. I have been discussing a broader range of topics before turning to this one. My purpose has been to make it clear that what the United States is doing in Central America is simply one typical expression of very general and longstanding features of its foreign policy. These features are easy to understand in terms of the structure of power within the United States. They are explained in the secret record of high-level planning and even much public discourse if one knows how to extract the real content from its rhetorical disguise. More significantly, these features are clearly revealed in the historical record, as the U.S. political leadership has proceeded to follow the advice of the doves, putting aside "vague" and "idealistic slogans" such as "human rights, the raising of the living standards, and democratization," and turning to harsh measures when necessary to achieve its "immediate national objectives," primary among them, to secure the Fifth Freedom.

In my opinion, one can gain an adequate understanding of what is happening right here in Central America only by approaching and thinking about the matter in this more general context. It is important to be clear about this, and not to fall into the error of supposing that current developments reflect some dramatically new departure in U.S. policy formation, some "blunder" or "deviation" that will be overcome by the choice of a new leadership within the political spectrum, which is, in reality, quite narrow. At the same time, I do not want to underestimate the differences that may exist within this spectrum. They are in fact rather limited, but in the case of a state with enormous power and resources of violence, slight changes may translate into very meaningful differences for the people at the wrong end of the guns.

I will turn now to Central America and the Caribbean, part of "our little region over here which never has bothered anybody," in the words of Secretary of War Henry Stimson in 1944, when he explained privately why it was entirely legitimate for the U.S. to maintain and extend its own regional system while dismantling those dominated by competitors and enemies. I will not focus specifically on the history and problems of Nicaragua, which you know much better than I, but on the region in general.

This "little region" has been under the effective control of the United States for a long time. Its history and current state therefore tell us a good deal about the United States. The picture is revealing, and not very pleasant to contemplate. The Central America-Caribbean region is one of the world's worst horror chambers, with rampant starvation, widespread conditions of virtual slave labor, torture, and massacre by U.S. clients. Efforts to bring about some constructive change have quite regularly called forth U.S. subversion or violence. It is an illuminating picture, one that could teach us North Americans a good deal about ourselves and our institutions, if we cared to learn—as of course we generally do not, because the lessons are of a sort that it is more comfortable not to understand.

A few weeks ago, the Washington-based Council on Hemispheric Affairs (COHA) published its annual Human Rights Report, covering 1985. It identified El Salvador and Guatemala as the two "worst" governments in Latin America; they were the "only two governments in this hemisphere that abducted, killed, and tortured political opponents on a systematic and widespread basis." This was the sixth consecutive year that El Salvador and Guatemala attained this honor, receiving "COHA's designation as the hemisphere's worst human rights offenders." During these six years, these two governments have been responsible for close to 150,000 civilian deaths, many with hideous torture and mutilation, and over two million refugees. The terror in Guatemala has continued in early 1986 since the inauguration of Vinicio Cerezo in January, with death squad killings actually increasing in these past weeks while the newly-elected President made it clear that he could do nothing, that "we have become the managers of bankruptcy and misery," in his words. In El Salvador too the killing goes on, though with so me changes as the situation has evolved. Human rights groups report that since President Duarte's election in 1984, "extrajudicial execution of non-combatant civilians, individual death squad-style killings, 'disappearances', arbitrary detention and torture" have been "taking place on a more selective basis against persons suspected of being in opposition to the present government or of being sympathetic to those that are" (Amnesty International). Last month, AI once again reported "convincing evidence that government agents routinely torture prisoners in their custody, conduct 'disappearances,' and commit political killings in attempts to eliminate opposition to the government . . . Most victims are non-combatant civilians, including women and children. In recent months troops have targeted refugee workers, trade unionists, and university staff and students for arrest, torture, and killing." Meanwhile, the toll of victims of the air war and murderous ground operations continues to mount.

In the conservative British journal *The Spectator*, correspondent Ambrose Evans-Pritchard explains the reasons for the changes that have occurred in the pattern of murder and torture in this client state. He reports an "improvement" in El Salvador: "Numbers are down and the bodies are dropped discreetly at night into the middle of Lake Ilopango and only rarely wash up onto the shore to remind bathers that the repression is still going on." This "improvement" results from the fact that "the war no longer requires" the earlier approach of indiscriminate slaughter: "The death squads did exactly what they were supposed to do: they decapitated the trade unions and mass organizations that seemed in danger of setting off an urban insurrection at the beginning of the decade," and now, following the directions of its U.S. military advisers, the army—in effect, a U.S. proxy army— is following the classic tactic implemented by the U.S. in its successful destruction of the South Vietnamese resistance: "to drive civilians out of the zones and leave the guerrillas cut off from their support structure. Without the 'sea' (people), wrote Chairman Mao, the 'fish' (guerrillas) cannot survive. So the sea must be drained." The peasants flee air attacks with 500-pound bombs and fragmentation bombs that "blast shrapnel in all directions," and then "the troops go through their villages, burning crops, killing livestock, tearing down houses, ripping up water pipes, and even planting hideous booby traps in the ruins they leave behind." The army, Evans-Pritchard continues, "learnt its tricks at American counter-insurgency schools in Panama and the United States. 'We learnt from you', a death squad member once told an American reporter, 'we learnt from you the methods, like blowtorches in the armpits, shots in the balls.' And political prisoners often insist they were tortured by foreigners, some Argentinian, others maybe American."

The careful observer will find that the worst atrocities have regularly been conducted by elite battalions fresh from their U.S. training. Salvadoran officers who admit their participation in death squad killings describe their service under CIA control and the training sessions on effective torture conducted by U.S. instructors. The significance of these facts cannot, however, be perceived in the West.

One other organization in Central America was in the competition for worst human rights offender of 1985, COHA reports,
as in earlier years: the contras attacking Nicaragua from their
Honduran and Costa Rican bases, a U.S. "proxy army" as even
its fervid enthusiasts concede in internal documents (Bruce
Cameron and Penn Kemble). Their achievements include hundreds if nor thousands of civilians murdered, tortured, and muti-
lated, with no other military operations of note. It is only their
more limited means, and the fact that the civilian population has
an army to protect it, that has kept the contras from matching
their counterparts in El Salvador and Guatemala. Human rights
investigators have compiled a rich compendium of horrors, occasionally reported in the United States when one of these studies
is released in Washington, then quickly forgotten, sometimes even
dismissed as "propaganda" by political figures and eminent Western intellectuals in the familiar style of apologists for state terror.
U.S. reporters for the major media somehow cannot seem to discover these atrocities, though the foreign press has no more difficulty than investigators for human rights groups. A high State
Department official concedes privately that the Department is
following a policy of "intentional ignorance" on this matter—as
are the mass media in the United States quite generally.

The exploits of these three champion human rights violators
are not just ordinary killing. The bare statistics do not convey
the true picture. The true picture in El Salvador is given by the
skulls and skeletons in the "body dump" at El Playón, or the
scene of women hanging from their feet, their breasts cut off
and facial skin peeled back, bleeding to death after the army has
passed through; and in Nicaragua, by an eyewitness account by
a North American priest, telling of a 14-year old girl, raped by
contras who then slit her throat, cut off her head and placed it
on a pole to intimidate others, to mention one all-too-typical example. In Guatemala, we gain a glimpse of the reality from the

reports of a few survivors of an army attack in Quiché province, where the army entered a village, rounded up the population in the town court house, decapitated the men, raped the women, and then killed the children by bashing their heads against the rocks of a nearby stream. This particular atrocity, again all-too-typical, was under the regime of General Ríos Montt, a man who was "totally dedicated to democracy" according to President Reagan and who had been falsely accused of complicity in atrocities, Reagan assured the public, joined by Jeane Kirkpatrick, Elliott Abrams, and other enthusiastic partisans of mass murder and brutal terror.

These three winners in the competition for "worst human rights violators" merit comparison to Pol Pot, a fact that will surprise North Americans who have been insulated from the facts. Furthermore, they are close U.S. allies—in the case of El Salvador and the contras, simply U.S. proxies, though in Guatemala it was necessary to call upon mercenary states (Argentina under the neo-Nazi generals, Israel, and others) after Congress had made it difficult for the U.S. government to participate in near-genocide as fully as it would have liked. To this toll we may add some 50,000 killed by Somoza's National Guard in its last paroxysm of fury in 1978-9. Contrary to many fables, Somoza was supported by the Carter Administration to the bloody end, until it was clear that he could no longer be maintained, at which point the U.S. strove to ensure that the National Guard would remain intact and effectively in power, the same strategy it pursued successfully with the collapse of the Romero dictatorship in El Salvador in the same year. When this tactic failed, the U.S. soon began to reconstitute the remnants of the National Guard as a proxy army in Honduran and Costa Rican sanctuaries—a "terrorist" force, in the terms of a secret "Weekly Intelligence Summary" of the Pentagon's Defense Intelligence Agency (July 16, 1982; leaked in 1984).

The U.S. commitment to its terrorist operations in Central America is no minor matter. The costs in 1985 alone may have amounted to some $10 billion when all elements are taken into account, more than the combined national budgets of the five Central American states.

This record also teaches us North Americans something about ourselves—or would, if we cared to learn.

Without wandering further through the chamber of horrors, let us return to the crucial question: What lies behind these quite systematic policies? I suggested a general answer in the first two lectures, but let us approach the question along a different path, inquiring into the "official explanation."

An answer to this question was provided by President John F. Kennedy, when he said that the United States would always prefer "a decent democratic regime," but—and this is a big "but"—if there is a danger of a Castro, then we will always support a Trujillo. The question then reduces to this: What exactly is "a Castro"? We will see that "a Castro" is not necessarily "a Communist" (whatever that term is supposed to mean) or "a Russian ally"; rather, the term designates a much broader category.

I will return directly to a closer examination of this very essential topic. As for what Kennedy meant by "a Trujillo," that is easy to answer. Trujillo was the murderous and brutal dictator of the Dominican Republic installed with U.S. support, who tortured, murdered and robbed with U.S. support for the next 30 years until the U.S. turned against him when his robbery extended to U.S. corporations and local elites associated with them and his exploits began to interfere with other U.S. terrorist operations in the region.

In fact, the Dominican Republic serves as an illuminating case study to help us answer the question: What is "a Castro"?

The first Marine landing in the Dominican Republic was in 1800. The more serious U.S. interventions, however, took place in this century, particularly under President Woodrow Wilson, the great apostle of self-determination, who celebrated this doctrine by invading Hispaniola among other exercises, as I mentioned earlier. In the Dominican Republic, his warriors fought for almost 6 years to subdue the "damned dagoes" (as his predecessor Theodore Roosevelt had called them). This vicious counterinsurgency war has virtually disappeared from American history. The first serious scholarly study devoted to it, by Bruce Calder, appeared after 60 years, in 1984; not coincidentally, this was a period of renewed concern over "our little region over here," as the situation appeared to be getting out of hand, with rising threats to the Fifth Freedom.

Calder regards the U.S. intervention as "a policy neither wise nor just, a policy basically unproductive for all concerned." Its consequences severe for the native population, beneficial to U.S. corporations were "unintended." Whatever one thinks of the interpretation, he does describe the facts, which are remote from the standard tales of U.S. benevolence that one reads in general histories and political science journals. Wilson invaded to block constitutional government and ensure complete U.S. economic and military control of the errant nation. The marines were "often brutish by Dominican standards," Calder continues. They murdered, destroyed villages, tortured, established concentration camps to provide a cheap labor force for sugar plantations, and in general, carried out brutal repression. The end result was that one-quarter of the agricultural land was in the hands of sugar companies, overwhelmingly U.S.-owned, while the population sank into misery and destitution.

These exercises, of course, were conducted strictly in "self-defense." There were no Bolsheviks available as a threat to national security at the time, so the U.S. was officially engaged in self-defense against the Huns. This stance was consistent with a long tradition, which we may trace back to "self-defense" against the "merciless Indian Savages" as described in the U.S. Declaration of Independence. The record includes "self-defense" against the Spaniards and the British through the 19th century, which necessitated massacre and expulsion of the native population during the conquest of the national territory; against a Mexican attack (launched deep inside Mexico) that led to the annexation of over one-third of Mexico; against Filipino "bandits," who had "assailed our sovereignty" as President McKinley angrily proclaimed; against the "internal aggression" of the South Vietnamese in the 1960s; and on and on.

In 1919, Dominican President Henriquez, who had been installed under Marine rule, went to the Versailles conference to plead for the right of self-determination that Wilson professed to champion. To no avail. Wilson succeeded in excluding consideration of U.S. hegemony in "our little region over here" from the proceedings at Versailles. Henriquez was not the only one to learn the true meaning of Wilson's exalted rhetoric. A young Vietnamese nationalist tried to approach him to present a petition requesting "permanent representation in the French Parliament by elected natives in order to keep it informed of native aspirations." But the Marines guarding Wilson chased him away "like a pest," one historian observes—an important phase in the education of the man later known as Ho Chi Minh.

The invaders left as one legacy the Dominican National Guard, and soon after, the dictatorship of its commander, Rafael Trujillo, who had joined the Guard in 1919 and took power in a military coup in 1930. Everything was just fine for almost 30 years. Trujillo was praised as a forward-looking leader by U.S. officials after such accomplishments as the massacre of some 20,000 Haitians in one month in 1937 along with regular barbarous treatment of the Dominicans themselves. Trujillo was "responsible for the great work of Dominican progress," the distinguished figure later to become Kennedy's Ambassador to the OAS proclaimed;

it was Trujillo, he said, "who brought trade between the Republic and the other American nations to a peak," meanwhile incidentally enriching U.S. investors.

By the late 1950s, however, Trujillo's corruption was beginning to infringe on the Fifth Freedom, as he took over about three-quarters of the economy for his own purposes. Furthermore, he was proving to be an impediment to the efforts of the Eisenhower and Kennedy Administrations to enlist the Latin American states in their anti-Castro crusade. He was assassinated in 1961, possibly with CIA complicity.* Democratic elections were held for the first time in 1962, and Juan Bosch assumed the presidency. He was basically a Kennedy liberal. The Kennedy Administration proceeded at once to undermine him. Aid was terminated, except for what had already been committed to the business-run Junta replaced in the democratic election. The U.S. Embassy demanded that the military structure of the Trujillo regime be retained intact—very much what Carter tried to accomplish after the fall of Somoza, and did accomplish in El Salvador a few months later, further evidence that little is new under the sun. The U.S. blocked the removal of Trujillist officers and prevented reform of the military, thus virtually guaranteeing a military coup unless Bosch could prevent it by mobilizing sufficient popular support through meaningful social reforms. The Kennedy Administration blocked agrarian reform and labor organization, with the aid of U.S. labor leaders, who have a dismal record of anti-labor activities in much of the world. The U.S. military retained its close contacts with Trujillist officers. Kennedy's Ambassador, John Bartlow Martin, complained that he was being treated as an outsider, whereas previously the government "seemed to feel that I was one of them" and followed the Embassy's prescriptions. Bosch fought corrup-

---

*See Piero Gleijeses, *The Dominican Crisis* (Baltimore: John Hopkins University Press, 1978) Appendix I, for an assessment of the evidence.

tion and defended civil liberties, a position that the Kennedy liberals found particularly outrageous because it meant that "Communists" and "Marxists" were granted civil rights, an intolerable affront to "democracy." He ended police repression and took steps to educate workers and peasants for democratic participation, thus instituting a "crisis of democracy," from the U.S. perspective. He also initiated an economic revival, geared to domestic needs and concerns. Obviously, we had to "let him go," in Ambassador Martin's phrase.

The inevitable military coup took place in 1963, recognized shortly after by the U.S. government, which offered it full support. CONATRAL, the union organized by the U.S. labor leadership which operates with funding provided by the U.S. government and in close coordination with private capital, praised the "patriotic gesture" of the armed forces in overthrowing Bosch. Earlier, CONATRAL had "called on the armed forces to defend the country against what it viewed as the communist menace," Jan Knippers Black observes in her recent study of the Dominican Republic.

Reviewing these events, historian Cole Blasier observes that "the United States failed in its objective of maintaining Bosch, a popularly elected president, in office in an orderly transition to a democratic system"; the "announced U.S. goal of promoting democracy. . .was subordinated to U.S. private and public vested interests," specifically, "concern for U.S. investors and traders." The latter comment is descriptively accurate; the former once again reflects the precepts of the ideological system. The "objective of maintaining Bosch" was as real as Woodrow Wilson's objective of bringing democracy and self-determination to the Dominican Republic 40 years earlier.

The result of the overthrow of Bosch's liberal democratic government was economic decline, a return to corruption and repression, and—crucially—an end to the "crisis of democracy" and threats to the Fifth Freedom. Everything was fine once again. There were no objections from the Ruler of the Hemisphere and little detectable concern elsewhere in the civilized world.

In short, Bosch was one of those "Castros" whom the U.S. must oppose in favor of a Trujillo. He was not a "Communist," but a liberal democrat, committed to reformist capitalist democracy, meaningful democracy with programs designed to serve domestic needs. His was one of those "nationalistic regimes" that serves the wrong "national interest." Correspondingly, he was intolerable to Big Brother.

The story continues. In 1965, a constitutionalist coup attempted to restore Bosch, the legally elected president, to office. Twenty-three thousand U.S. Marines were dispatched to block this threat to "stability" under a series of pretexts too absurd to merit comment. The Marines fought against the popularly supported constitutionalist forces, then stood by passively while the Dominican military whom they had rescued carried out a slaughter of civilians. To intervene at this point would have violated U.S. neutrality, the government explained.

This time, the consequences were still more severe: death squads, torture, mass starvation, the flight of hundreds of thousands of people to the United States—and outstanding opportunities for U.S. investors, who bought up most of the rest of the country, led by the conglomerate Gulf & Western, a major corporation with substantial influence in the U.S. government and annual sales surpassing the gross national product of the Dominican Republic. G&W took over much of the domestic economy and the agricultural land, producing sugar and other crops for export while local food consumption declined. Sugar production was, at the time, highly profitable thanks to the destruction of independent unions and the availability of starving Haitians who worked as virtual slaves, leased for this purpose by the Haitian dictatorship or fleeing the incredible poverty in their own native land.

By 1970, the rate of political murders was higher than under Trujillo. The country recorded economic growth while wages declined through the 1970s with labor "pacified," never to recover the status it had briefly begun to attain during the Bosch years. Constitutional barriers to foreign ownership of land were removed and U.S. aid financed infrastructure projects for the benefit of investors, primarily North American.

With the country utterly demoralized and firmly under the control of the security forces and U.S. corporations, the U.S. was willing to tolerate "free elections," even the election of social democrats, all possibility of social reform or democracy having been terminated. The economic catastrophe continued. In 1985, the Dominican Bishops conference warned that "the foundations of Dominican society are disintegrating as a result of a crisis that has plagued the country for years," with "inhuman and unjust poverty" for much of the population, 90% of whom suffered malnutrition according to Central Bank officials. "The situation of underdevelopment and poverty is not the result of coincidence," the Bishops observed, but "it is the consequence of concrete economic social and political structures," namely, those initiated and maintained by regular U.S. intervention to ensure that "stability" is not threatened. By the latter part of the 1970s the artificial economy began to collapse as a consequence of the general world economic crisis. The social democratic political leadership, a pale reflection of the Bosch years, responded by expanding the bureaucracy and bribing the military to prevent a military coup, while cutting back programs that might benefit the poor and the already miserable social services. With prices increasing and standards of living declining still further under conditions imposed by the International Monetary Fund (IMF), popular unrest increased, leading to the killing of 100 demonstrators by elite U.S.-trained counterinsurgency forces in 1984. Shortly after, the Reagan Administration cut back the Dominican sugar quota, a further blow to a country dependent on the U.S. market now that any hope of independent development had been aborted.

At best, there is little that any government could now do in the Dominican Republic. As Jan Black accurately summarizes the situation, if some government "reaches out beyond the parameters drawn by the IMF, the United States, certain business interests, and the armed forces to respond to the urgent needs of the poor majority, it runs the risk of being overthrown." That is the clear lesson of history in this corner of "our little region."

This glorious record is regarded as a grand success in the United States, even a proof of U.S. benevolence. "No Dominican could doubt but that his country was a far, far better place to live in 1922 than it was in 1916" when Wilson landed the Marines, the respected Harvard political scientist Samuel Huntington confidently asserts in the *Political Science Quarterly*. The U.S. "deserves a lion's share of the credit" for having "nurtured the development of democratic institutions in the Dominican Republic," he continues, a sparkling demonstration of how "the overall effect of American power on other societies was to further liberty, pluralism, and democracy." Other distinguished figures have chimed in with similar praise for this long-term exercise in what historian Arthur Schlesinger once described as "our general program of international goodwill."

So effectively has the system of indoctrination worked its miracles that U.S. observers are continually shocked at the attitudes of the benighted natives. In April 1981, the U.S. Navy landed in a "goodwill visit" to commemorate the Marine landing of April 1965, setting off a wave of demonstrations and police atrocities and killings. At a news conference called by the visiting U.S. Admiral to reiterate "the friendly nature of the visit" and to stress the "common threat" posed by the Soviet Union to both the U.S. and the Dominican Republic, "a Dominican reporter observed that the Soviet Union had never invaded the Dominican Republic but that the United States had done so twice," the reporter for the *New York Times* observed. She adds that the vehemence of the opposition to the goodwill visit "caught Dominican leaders and American officials by surprise"—but says nothing about the U.S. role in creating the horrifying conditions of poverty and destitution that she discovered in neighborhoods "papered with posters saying 'Yankee get out'"—an inexplicable reaction to so many years of U.S. care and solicitude.

Perhaps the history of U.S. intervention in the Dominican Republic is an aberration, a departure from U.S. principles and norms of international behavior and thus not really a fair example of these principles and norms. We can quickly disabuse ourselves of such notions by reviewing the record elsewhere in "our little region over here which has never bothered anybody." Let us consider a few examples.

President Wilson also sent the Marines to Haiti, where they carried out a counterinsurgency campaign against the "niggers" (in the terminology of the day, from top government officials to the soldier in the field) even more savage than in the neighboring Dominican Republic, murdering, destroying and reinstituting virtual slave labor in a war imbued with vicious racism, and again leaving the country in the hands of the National Guard after a 20-year military occupation, to be followed from the 1950s by the Duvalier dictatorship. "Papa Doc" and his successor "Baby Doc," who took over in 1971, were kept in power by a private army, the Tontons Macoutes, who may have killed as many as 100,000 people—in the style of the Salvadoran and Guatemalan security forces—under the regime of "Baby Doc" alone, the exiled head of the Haitian Center for Human Rights believes. All this was surely well-known to the U.S. government. There is good reason to believe that the U.S. trained these forces, who also worked closely with Haitian and U.S. businesses to enforce company terms on workers. The U.S. military mission trained and equipped their successors, the army shock troops called the Leopards, whose current task is to enforce "Duvalierism without Duvalier" after the collapse of the U.S.-backed regime. According to the World Bank, 3800 families own 80% of the national wealth in this country of about 6 million people; 87% of children suffer malnutrition; there is 82% illiteracy; 60% of the population have an annual per capita income of $60 or less. Torture, state terror, grinding poverty, and conditions approximating slavery are the common lot. Haiti is a disaster in human and ecological terms, the poorest country in the Hemisphere, perhaps beyond hope of recovery.

This episode too is considered a great tribute to U.S. benevolence. The noted Harvard historian David Landes, discussing the terrible history and condition of Haiti, writes that "the only period of relative tranquillity was the 20 years of American presence," as the Marines "helped keep order, improved communications, and provided the stability needed to make the political system work and to facilitate trade with the outside." But as elsewhere so often, U.S. benevolence was unappreciated, he notes: "even a benevolent occupation creates resistance, though, not only among the beneficiaries, but also among the more enlightened members of the dominant society."

Hewson Ryan, Professor of Public Diplomacy at the renowned Fletcher School of Law and Diplomacy at Tufts University goes still further. "Few nations have been the object over such a sustained period of so much well-intentioned guidance and support as Haiti," he writes. We can learn a good deal about the U.S. ideological system, which is remarkable in its effectiveness, by a closer look at the evidence for this benevolence offered by this distinguished commentator.

Much of our diplomatic activity during the 19th century, Ryan writes, "was directed at protecting [Haiti's] territorial integrity from European invasions, or from attempts by Haitian politicians to compromise their nation by sales or concessions of land," surely a noble endeavor—undertaken at a time when the U.S. was not yet powerful enough to take over the region for itself and was confined to limiting European incursions. Ryan does not proceed to discuss what happened when the U.S. had effectively displaced its European rivals. The answer is given by the reaction of the State Department to a Haitian draft of a proposed constitution, submitted under the Marine occupation in 1916. It would not do, the Department observed, because it had "unprogressive" features, among them clauses forbidding the alienation of Haitian territory to foreigners-that is, U.S. investors, primarily. A new constitution was therefore written and imposed by the occupiers, eliminating such "unprogressive" features. Franklin Delano Roosevelt later boasted that he was the author of the Haitian constitution. So much for the noble effort to protect Haiti from sales or concessions of land to foreigners.

Ryan tells us that during the Marine "occupation" (he gives the word in quotes, implying that no effort so benign could properly be described in these terms), "Haiti was the recipient of all manner of well-intentioned technical assistance," such as "a modern highway network." "Nor was the formal political aspect neglected" by the philanthropists tending selflessly to Haiti's needs, he observes. As evidence, he cites Roosevelt's pride in his "feat" of drafting "the new Haitian constitution," while ignoring the contents of this document and the background, just mentioned. As for the "well-intentioned technical assistance," Professor Ryan spares us the details, for example, the use of slave labor to build the highways at remarkably low cost. He also spares the reader the facts about the vicious racism of the occupiers, their brutality, the thousands murdered during ruthless suppression of Haitian rebellions, and so on, and even has the effrontery to state, without irony, that "the Duvalier dynasty. . .itself might be seen as having at least some of its roots in U.S. well-intentioned intervention." As these examples illustrate, there are few limits to the capacity of respected

Western intellectuals to interpret brutality, atrocities and racist horrors as exemplifying the highest values and noblest intentions.

Haiti merited little notice in the United States or the community of civilized nations until the past few weeks. It is not that nothing was happening there. Surely events were occurring that might have caused some mild interest among the Western humanists who are so profoundly distressed by real or alleged human rights abuses in Nicaragua (post-Somoza, of course), which is by a considerable margin the major focus of such concerns in "our little region" within the U.S. media, not to speak of the Reagan Administration, which devotes more space to human rights violations in Nicaragua than in any other country in the world in the State Department's Country Reports on Human Rights Practices for 1985 (violations that are largely fabricated, as Americas Watch demonstrates in its review of this sordid document).

For example, in June 1985 the Haitian legislature unanimously adopted a new law governing political parties. It required that every political party must recognize in its statutes President-for-Life Jean-Claude Duvalier as the supreme arbiter of the nation, outlawed any party with a connection to any religion (hence the Christian Democratic Party), and granted the Minister of Interior and Defense the right to suspend the rights of any political party without reason. The law was ratified by a popular vote of 99.98% approval. The new electoral law did not pass without a reaction from the United States. The U.S. Ambassador, speaking at a reception on the annual July 4th celebration of U.S. independence, informed the assembled guests that the new law was "an encouraging step forward " and called for "dialogue" to permit the establishment of new parties in conformity with it. The Administration continued to certify to Congress that "democratic development" is progressing in Haiti, so that military and economic aid could continue to flow uninterrupted (mainly, into the pockets of Baby Doc and his family and friends). In October 1985, the Reagan Administration once again reported that human rights had improved. Aid to Haiti more than doubled during the 1980s, in accord with the basic principle of U.S. policy proclaimed by the House Foreign Affairs Committee: "to maintain friendly relations with Duvalier's non-Communist government." The Reagan Administration was quite pleased with developments in Haiti, particularly, because it had been able to reach an agreement with Haiti permitting the U.S. to stop and return boat people trying to flee to refuge in the United States, by armed force if necessary; more than 3000 had been returned under this arrangement by the end of 1984. Concern over these developments ranged from slight to nonexistent, as is always the case when order reigns and profits flow.

By December, there were signs that all was not well. There was increased turbulence, demonstrations and killing by the security forces. It was becoming clear that the U.S.-supported dictatorship was facing problems. Here is the way the *Wall Street Journal* (Feb. 10, 1986) describes what happened next:

> An administration official said that the White House concluded late last year, following huge demonstrations that hadn't been seen on such a scale before, that the regime was unraveling. After Mr. Duvalier made major cabinet changes last December, U.S. analysts learned that Haiti's ruling inner circle had lost faith in the 34-year-old president for life. As a result, U.S. officials, including Secretary of State George Shultz, began openly calling for a "democratic process" in Haiti.
> Before that, everything was quite satisfactory.

The cynicism is extraordinary, but passes without notice in a highly indoctrinated society. And the Reagan Administration now receives awed acclaim for its positive role in removing Duvalier when his rule could no longer be maintained, just as it did when it turned against Marcos a few weeks later under similar circumstances, when it became clear that he could no longer perform his assigned tasks. All of this teaches us something about the profound concern for the "democratic process" that occasionally becomes a priority for Shultz and others, under interesting circumstances.

Haiti, then, must be another "aberration," alongside of the Dominican Republic, another case where the best of intentions unaccountably went astray. There are other cases as well in "our little region over here"—as elsewhere.

Twenty years before the U.S. "furthered liberty, pluralism and democracy" in Hispaniola and provided "relative tranquillity" to the ungrateful "beneficiaries" of its efforts there, the U.S. fought the Spanish-American war for "fundamentally humanitarian motives" (Harvard historian Frank Freidel). The chief of the bureau of foreign commerce at the U.S. Department of Commerce, writing in 1902, had a slightly different and somewhat more realistic view of these "humanitarian motives":

> Underlying the popular sentiment, which might have evaporated in time, which forced the United States to take up arms against Spanish rule in Cuba, were our economic relations with the West Indies and the South American republics. So strong was this commercial instinct that had there been no emotional cause, such as the alleged enormities of Spanish rule or the destruction of the *Maine*, we would have doubtless taken steps in the end to abate with a strong hand what seemed to be an economic nuisance. . .The Spanish-American War was but an incident of a general movement of expansion which had its root in the changed environment of an industrial capacity far beyond our domestic powers of consumption. It was seen to be necessary for us not only to find foreign purchasers for our goods, but to provide the means of making access to foreign markets easy, economical and safe.

In fact, Cuba had long been regarded as a "ripe fruit" that could be plucked by the United States when the proper time had come. In 1823, Secretary of State John Quincy Adams urged that the U.S. support Spanish sovereignty over Cuba until it would fall into U.S. hands by "the laws of political . . . gravitation." I mentioned earlier Thomas Jefferson's similar thoughts about Spanish rule in Latin America. It took some time, but these laws were operating as anticipated 75 years later, as Cuban nationalist rebels approached victory in their long struggle against Spanish occupation. But the U.S. had other ideas in mind. U.S. intervention removed Spanish rule while effectively blocking Cuban independence and extending to the "liberated" society the benefits of the Fifth Freedom, turning Cuba into the very prototype of a "neo-colony."

A leading Wall Street banker had written in 1898 that "The United States must absolutely occupy Cuba, and hold it under military rule until the people are prepared for a self-government that will be satisfactory to this country [the U.S.]": the usual concept of "democracy." The plans of the Cuban insurgents were plainly unacceptable, with their call for Cuban independence and universal suffrage, meaning participation by peasants and workers, many of them Blacks-effectively disenfranchised in the U.S., and surely not to be given a voice in the fate of their country in this "ripe fruit" that was now finally ready for harvest.

The U.S. media and the political and military leadership generally agreed. The presumption that Cubans were prepared for self-government was "false and insubstantial," the *New York Tribune* declared, adding that too many of them were "ignorant niggers, half-breeds and dagoes." One divisional commander of the U.S. expeditionary force, General S.B.M. Young, described the insurgents as "a lot of degenerates, absolutely devoid of honor or gratitude, . . . no more capable of self-government than the savages of Africa," and the commander of the expeditionary force, General William Shafter, rejected the Cuban claim for self-government with contempt, observing, not inaccurately, that "we have taken Spain's war upon ourselves." U.S. proconsul Leonard Wood claimed that "the propertied classes, and all the foreigners in Cuba, including the Spaniards"—as distinct from the "degenerates"—favored annexation to the U.S. The U.S. took over in alliance with these groups, mainly conservatives who had opposed the Cuban revolution, very much the pattern of the post-World War II period, as we have seen. The U.S. proceeded to establish what Wood called "a firm and stable government in the hands of men who would not hesitate to use severe measures should the occasion arise." Such measures should suffice, Wood felt, to handle the Cubans, "a quiet people," he explained, "without enough force of character to be seriously troublesome if we can only keep them moderately busy," though it was also necessary to resort to such devices as public horsewhipping of Cubans who opposed his policies. More generally Wood explained, "in dealing with the Latin races it is not advisable to yield under pressure, unless one is prepared to give up everything and submit to be ruled." Hence firmness is necessary if the Latin races become troublesome and do not remember their proper place.

This alliance of the U.S., the propertied classes and Spanish elites laid the basis for the takeover of Cuban land and resources by U.S. corporations, who turned the country into a U.S. plantation, its prospects of independent development terminated, conditions that Cuba has yet to escape.

Years earlier, Cuban nationalist leader Jose Marti, who had long feared U.S. intervention, asked: "Once the United States is in Cuba, who will get it out?" When the "liberation" of Cuba from Spain had been consummated, Maximo Gomez, who had fought courageously as the leader of the revolt against Spain, told an American reporter that "Cuba fought against the dominion of Spain only to find herself under the heel of the United States." An accurate judgment.

The U.S. at once turned to the Philippines, destroying the antiquated and defenseless Spanish fleet and then "defending" the country from its own population at a fearful cost, with consequences that remain grim 85 years later.

Cuba posed few problems until the 1930s, when Franklin Delano Roosevelt's Administration celebrated the Good Neighbor policy by overturning the civilian government of Dr. Ramon Grau San Martin, regarded as a possible threat to U.S. commercial interests, in favor of Fulgencio Batista. His military dictatorship enjoyed firm U.S. support and reciprocated by permitting the free exercise of the Fifth Freedom until it was overthrown in 1959 by Fidel Castro's forces. As always, Cuban attitudes towards the U.S. seemed inexplicable. President Eisenhower described his puzzlement over the hostility shown to the U.S. by Castro, whom U.S. Ambassador Bonsai described as an "abnormal man"—how else could one explain his attitude towards the Great Benefactor? In August 1959, Eisenhower said:

> I do feel. . .here is a country that you would believe, on the basis of our history, would be one of our real friends. . .the trade concessions we have made, and the very close relationships that have existed. . .make it a puzzling matter to figure out just exactly why the Cubans and the Cuban government would be so unhappy when, after all, their principal market is right here. . . . I don't know exactly what the difficulty is.

Given the evident irrationality of any Cuban animus towards its long-term benefactor, it must be that the Communists are at work, poisoning the friendly relations of 60 years.

Notice that the puzzlement in the United States over Cuban attitudes is, once again, a testimony to the effective workings of the U.S. system of indoctrination and thought control over many years, as already illustrated in the case of Haiti and the Dominican Republic.

By December 1959, the CIA had begun to organize a Cuban exile army and a few months later, CIA chief Allen Dulles reported to Eisenhower that Castro posed as great a danger to "mutual security" as had Jacobo Arbenz, whose democratic government in Guatemala had been removed in a successful CIA coup 6 years earlier. Then came the Bay of Pigs invasion, and the terrorist war against Cuba launched by the Kennedy Administration. Cuba was the prime victim of international terrorism for the next 20 years, probably surpassing the rest of the world combined, if we exclude from the category of terrorism cases that might more properly be called outright aggression, such as Israel's bombing of Lebanon with U.S. support from the early 1970s. Nicaragua has since taken over first place as the U.S. launched its terrorist war to abort "the threat of a good example" there, shortly after the failure to preserve National Guard rule in 1979—though we might again assign these actions to the category of outright aggression, and one might argue that state terrorism in El Salvador by what amounts to a U.S. mercenary army counts as international terrorism, in which case this country receives the prize for the 1980s.

While taking over Cuba from Spain, the U.S. also invaded Puerto Rico with the intent of holding the island as a permanent U.S. possession. Puerto Rican independence fighters were kept out of San Juan during the Spanish surrender, just as Cuban insurgents were forbidden to enter Santiago as the war against Spain ended or to sign the surrender, and Filipino fighters were excluded from Manila though 12,000 had taken part in the capture of the city. The reasoning was explained by the Navy Department in the last case, though it holds throughout: a political alliance with the insurgents would enable them "to maintain their cause in the future," an unacceptable consequence.

Puerto Rico too was turned into a sugar plantation for the benefit of U.S. agribusiness, virtually eliminating native agriculture. Later, an industrialization strategy based on tax exemptions and other incentives led to industrial growth for export. By Third World standards, Puerto Rico ranks high in terms of per capita income, life expectancy and the like. The other side of the coin is that 40% of the population have emigrated to urban slums in the United

States (at a rate that reached its peak in the 1980s), farmlands are virtually abandoned, 60% of the population are dependent on food stamps and most of the rest work in foreign-owned factories or government offices supported by the U.S. government. Two-thirds of the adult population do not work at all; the population survives by "massive transfers and a two-way emigrant stream," economist Richard Weisskoff observes in a recent study, noting that the Puerto Rican economy "consumes but does not produce. . .In short, the U.S. public underwrites the Puerto Rican people, while U.S. corporations shift profits through their Puerto Rican plants and back to the United States, tax free." This "great industrial strength," he adds, "is based on a tax gimmick that is also subject to revision. Much of the economic survival of Puerto Rico is due to pecuniary advantages, to fiscal or international bookkeeping rules that, if changed, can bring on more hardship" to a "bankrupt, dismembered economy heavily dependent on welfare."

Puerto Rico reveals clearly one of the features of imperialism often obscured by misleading and deceptive talk about "national interest" and other mystifications of the ideological system. An analysis of imperial systems reveals costs as well as profits, perhaps often comparable in scale, some studies indicate. Why then should great powers seek to control an empire (classical or neocolonial)? In terms of the mysticism of "national interest," the policy seems to make little sense. It makes a good deal of sense, however, when we reflect that the costs are social costs while the benefits are private benefits. The costs of the British Navy, or the U.S. military system, or food stamps to control popular dissidence in Puerto Rico, and so on, are paid by the general population of the imperial society. The profits go to investors, exporters, banks, commercial institutions, agribusiness and the like. The empire is just one of the many devices by which the poor subsidize the wealthy in the home society. Much the same is true of "aid," generally a form of export promotion or development for eventual

corporate profits. There is some truth to the familiar adage that
aid is a device whereby the poor in the wealthy societies subsidize
the wealthy in the poor societies, though more must be added:
like the imperial systems in general, it is also a device whereby
the poor in the wealthy societies enrich the wealthy at home—
with bits "trickling down" to the general population, when this
secondary condition can be satisfied.

Turning from the Caribbean to Central America, in El Salvador U.S. ships stood offshore as General Hernandez Martinez
conducted the 1932 *Matanza*, killing thousands of peasants—perhaps 30,000, some estimate—in a few weeks. "It was found unnecessary for the United States forces and British forces to land," the
U.S. Chief of Naval Operations testified before Congress, "as the
Salvadoran Government had the situation well in hand." Martinez
was duly recognized by the Roosevelt Administration in another
exercise of the Good Neighbor Policy, after winning an "election"
in which he was the only candidate, the political opposition having
been eliminated or suppressed. Everything was just fine in El Salvador too, in one of the world's most miserable countries, until
1960-1, when the U.S. sponsored a right-wing military coup to
block another potential threat to the Fifth Freedom, in accord with
President Kennedy's doctrine that "governments of the civil-mili-
tary type of El Salvador are the most effective in containing Communist penetration in Latin America." We return to the aftermath.

In Nicaragua, the first major U.S. military operation took
place in 1854, when the U.S. Navy burned down the port town
of San Juan del Norte to avenge an alleged insult to American
officials and the millionaire entrepreneur Cornelius Vanderbilt.
Marines landed in 1909 and again in 1912, establishing a military
occupation that lasted (apart from one year) until 1933, leading
to the establishment of the Somoza dictatorship after a murderous counterinsurgency campaign and the assassination of
Sandino by a ruse. The bloody and corrupt rule of the Somoza

dynasty lasted until 1979, with full U.S. support, while Somoza turned his country into a base for the projection of U.S. power in the region. President Carter's failure to maintain "Somocismo without Somoza" led to the reconstitution of the National Guard and the ongoing efforts to convert Honduras into the major U.S. military base for terrorizing the region, including the war of the U.S. proxy army against Nicaragua. The Sandinista revolution led to a sudden concern for "democracy" and "human rights" in Nicaragua among U.S. elites, a miraculous transformation that would be dismissed with the ridicule it deserves in societies less fully indoctrinated than those of the West.

In the case of Nicaragua too, U.S. elites find it difficult to understand the hostility expressed by the beneficiaries of their historical programs of "international goodwill." An explanation is provided by the respected liberal commentator William Shannon, former U.S. Ambassador to Ireland and now Distinguished Professor at Boston University. The fact that the Sandinistas "hate America," he writes, "is understandable given their limited education and their years spent in exile, in prison, or in the hills battling what they perceived as an American-backed dictatorship." Ignorant of the actual history of U.S. benevolence, they use anti-Americanism to provide "the energy for their political movement, much as anti-Semitism provided the energy for Nazism."

These are only a few examples; the more general picture is much the same. Returning to the choice among Kennedy's three policy options—"a decent democratic regime," "a Castro regime," and "a Trujillo regime," always to be preferred if there is a danger of "a Castro"—recall the first case we considered, the record of U.S. intervention in the Dominican Republic, no aberration, as we have seen in this brief review. This history, and others like it, help us to understand John F. Kennedy's official answer to our question: what is the source of the systematic behavior of the U.S., illustrated today in El Salvador and Nicaragua? Democracy

NOAM CHOMSKY

is fine, but only if its results conform to the needs of Big Brother. If these needs are threatened by "a Castro"—for example, steps towards meaningful democracy under a democratic capitalist regime committed to social reform and independence—then we call out the death squads. The pattern is systematic, a systematic expression of the basic principles of foreign policy: specifically, the sanctity of the Fifth Freedom.

The Kennedy Administration followed this line of reasoning to the hilt. In 1962, the Administration made a decision which, in terms of its consequences, is one of the most significant of modern history. The mission of the Latin American military was to be changed from "hemispheric defense" to "internal security." "Hemispheric defense" was something of a joke; there was no one to defend the hemisphere against except the United States, and that was not what was intended. But "internal security" is no joke. It means war against the indigenous population. The result was a rash of National Security States reminiscent in several respects of European fascism, sometimes employing the talents of Nazi war criminals such as Klaus Barbie who had been brought to Latin America by the U.S. after their service in postwar Europe, a reign of vast terror, high-technology torture, "disappearances" and death squads. The first major coup was in Brazil, backed and welcomed by the U.S. government, which hailed it as "the single most decisive victory of freedom in the mid-twentieth century" (Assistant Secretary of State for Inter-American Affairs Lincoln Gordon). The domestic result was an "economic miracle" that was a disaster for most of the population, not to speak of the human rights catastrophe. There was also a domino effect throughout the region. The establishment of the Brazilian National Security State helped set off a "plague of repression" without parallel in the history of the continent, as described by a later high-level Commission headed by Sol Linowitz, which, however failed to trace all of this to its source.

In El Salvador, the Kennedy Administration established the basic structure of the death squads that were to sow terror on an unprecedented scale when they were put into operation in later years. In Guatemala, where the reformist capitalist democracy of Arévalo and Arbenz had been overthrown in a CIA coup in 1954, instituting 30 years of bloodshed and terror, the Kennedy Administration supported a military coup to prevent the threat of a democratic election in which, it was feared, Arévalo might be permitted to take part; like Bosch, he and his successor Arbenz were "Castros" who had to be rejected in favor of "a Trujillo." This led to a huge massacre in the latter part of the decade, with perhaps some 10,000 killed in a counterinsurgency campaign with direct participation of U.S. Green Berets and, it was reported, U.S. planes carrying out napalm raids from their Panamanian bases. This slaughter, however, pales in comparison to the state terrorism organized and supported by the United States in Central America in later years, reaching its peak of horror in the early 1980s.

The apparatus of repression and torture established by the Kennedy Administration was an integral component of Kennedy's Alliance for Progress. This program, much lauded as a display of U.S. benevolence, was utterly cynical in conception. It was not motivated by a sudden discovery of suffering and poverty in Latin America but rather by fear of the "contagion" that might spread from the Cuban "virus." As in the case of Southeast Asia, which I discussed in the last lecture, this danger required a two-pronged effort; first, destruction of the virus at its source (invasion, embargo, and a 20-year terrorist war); and second, steps to inoculate the region from infection. The Alliance for Progress was designed as the "hearts and minds" component of the second project, to be pursued alongside of the measures to ensure "internal security."

But the Alliance for Progress itself required harsh measures. The Alliance was designed to foster economic development, but

of a special kind, a kind that is fully in accord with the requirements of the Fifth Freedom. Development was to be geared to
production for export. The aid flowed, bur with the usual beneficiaries: U.S. agribusiness, fertilizer and pesticide companies,
and local elites associated with them. Statistically, there were
some impressive results. Thus, beef production increased in all
of the Central American countries. Meanwhile, however, beef
consumption generally declined—radically, in Costa Rica and El
Salvador and noticeably in Guatemala and Nicaragua—as beef
was produced for export. The same processes reduced food supplies for local needs as crop lands were converted to production
of beef and commercial crops, while valuable forest lands were
destroyed with long-term effects that are incalculable, in the interest of foreign corporations, their domestic clients, and the
wealthy minority that could purchase imported food and luxury
goods. Like the "economic miracle" in the Dominican Republic
and Brazil, the Alliance recorded statistical growth in Central
America alongside of increased misery and starvation for much
of the population. This development model has a necessary
corollary: it requires an apparatus of repression to control the inevitable dissidence and resistance as its consequences are en-
dured by the subject population. Death squads are not an
accidental counterpart to the Alliance for Progress, but an essential component. It is therefore not surprising that the apparatus of repression was put into place, to be ready when needed,
as the Alliance for Progress was initiated.

We gain some further insight into Kennedy's answer to our
question by a look at the recent history of El Salvador. Elections
were held there in 1972. When it became clear that the victors
would be José Napoleón Duarte and Guillermo Ungo, the military stepped in to take over with blatant fraud and intervention
by Guatemala and Somoza, who played the same role he filled
in providing a base for the abolition of democracy in Guatemala

by the CIA in 1954 and helping to prevent the reconstitution of the democratically-elected government in the Dominican Republic in 1965, and in the Bay of Pigs invasion in 1961. Duarte was taken prisoner and tortured. After his release, he came to Washington, where neither the press nor Congress (with two exceptions) could be troubled even to speak to him.

This episode reveals with utter clarity the loathing of U.S. elites for democracy as long as everything is under control, and the cynicism of the current pretense of interest in "elections" as a thin cover for state terrorism.

Another electoral farce in 1977 passed in a similar manner. Meanwhile, torture, murder, repression and corruption proceeded in their normal way, arousing only limited interest and no serious reaction in the U.S.

Two problems, however, did begin to cause grave concern. The first was the impending overthrow of the Somoza regime. It was feared that Salvadoran dictator Romero might go the same way. In Nicaragua, the U.S. failed in its effort to impose "Somocismo without Somoza," the usual technique when some client is no longer useful or salvageable. The Carter Administration was determined not to repeat the same error in El Salvador.

The second problem was still more serious. The 1970s witnessed the growth of popular organizations in El Salvador on an impressive scale: Church-based self-help groups, peasant associations, teachers unions, and others. That is always a serious danger sign. It means that a basis is being laid for meaningful democracy in which the population at large may be able to participate in shaping public policy, hence a "crisis of democracy" and a threat to the system of elite decision, public ratification, called "democracy" in Western Newspeak. It is a truism that isolated individuals cannot confront concentrated power alone in the political arena, or elsewhere. They can enter the political arena only if they have ways to pool their limited resources, to discover relevant facts and to exchange information, to develop ideas and programs and act to realize them. When such means and organizational forms are lacking, democracy reduces to a game played among elite groups who command the resources that permit them to be active participants in the political system. The growth of popular organizations in El Salvador was therefore no trifling matter, but a development with potentially serious consequences if the rot were to be established and to spread.

In February 1980, Archbishop Romero wrote a letter to President Carter, pleading with him not to send military aid to the Junta who "know only how to repress the people and defend the interests of the Salvadoran oligarchy." The aid, he wrote to Carter, "will surely increase injustice here and sharpen the repression that has been unleashed against the people's organizations fighting to defend their most fundamental human rights."

The very essence of U.S. policy, however, was to destroy the people's organizations fighting to defend their most fundamental human rights. President Carter therefore sent the military aid with a message to Congress saying that it was intended "to strengthen the army's key role in reforms"—a phrase that would have made Orwell gasp.

The consequences were exactly as the Archbishop had predicted. In March, Archbishop Romero was assassinated, as the death squads went into action. A State of Siege was instituted, renewed monthly since, and in May the war against the peasantry was launched in full force under the guise of land reform. Peasants were the main victims of the Carter-Duarte war in 1980—not surprisingly, since "the masses were with the guerrillas" when this exercise began, Duarte later conceded.

The first major atrocity was the Río Sumpul massacre, when 600 fleeing peasants were slaughtered in a joint operation of the Salvadoran and Honduran armies. Eyewitnesses described how babies were thrown into the air for target practice, children decapitated, women tortured and drowned. José Napoleón Duarte, who had joined the junta in March in an effort to provide it with some legitimacy during the slaughter then being set in motion, justified the Río Sumpul massacre as legitimate because the victims were all "Communists"—including, presumably, the infants cut to pieces with machetes. The U.S. media suppressed the story for over a year, then gave it only passing mention and have yet to report it adequately, though very credible evidence was immediately available at once and it was reported in the international press and the Church-based press in the United States.

In June, the University was attacked with many killed; laboratories and libraries were destroyed, and another threat to order was eliminated. In November, the political opposition was executed by the security forces. Meanwhile the independent media were eliminated. The Church radio station was bombed and destroyed, the editor of one paper was found hacked to pieces and another fled after repeated assassination attempts. The basis was laid for "free elections," duly conducted under Reagan in an atmosphere of "terror and despair, macabre rumor and grisly reality," in the words of Lord Chitnis, who led the observers of the British Parliamentary Human Rights Group.

The U.S. media predictably hailed this triumph of democracy, and in later years, as the task of "decapitating" and destroying the popular organizations began to achieve notable success, U.S. commentators across the mainstream political spectrum registered their pleasure and approval of this exercise in "building democracy." They were not alone in taking this stance. Thus, a Dutch government commission observing the election, while conceding that "the parries of the left were excluded to a certain extent from the election process," concluded that "there was a sufficient range of choice for the voters." The phrase "excluded to a certain extent " refers to the program of mass slaughter, torture and disappearance, and the conception of a "sufficient range of choice" expresses well the concept of "democracy" widely held among Western elites. The Dutch Commission adds that, like Nicaragua, El Salvador is "embroiled in a civil war in which foreign intervention plays a major role," with the guerrillas "actively supported by foreign agencies. "This analogy merits no comment among sane people, but again gives a certain insight into the moral and intellectual level of Western elites.

On October 26, 1980, the martyred Archbishop's successor, Bishop Rivera y Damas, condemned the armed forces' "war of extermination and genocide against a defenseless civilian population." A few weeks later, Duarte hailed the same armed forces for their "valiant service alongside the people against subversion" as he was sworn in as President of the Junta in an effort to keep the military aid flowing to the killers after the murder of four American churchwomen, an act considered criminal in the United States. This has been Duarte's role throughout. No single figure in Latin American history has presided over a comparable slaughter; the numbers reach some 40,000, at a rather conservative estimate, during the period when he served to legitimize the atrocities and ensure that the U.S. contribution to them would be sufficient for the task at hand. Not surprisingly, he is the darling of the U.S. media and commentators, regarded as a great democrat and paragon of virtue.

Reagan took over in early 1981. The massacres escalated in sadism and scale, with direct U.S. participation as the U.S. Air Force undertook surveillance missions and coordination of bombing strikes, much improving the kill rate among fleeing peasants and defenseless villagers. These horrors, which continue, were greeted with mounting applause in the United States as the terror seemed to be achieving some success. The death toll is well over 60,000, with over a million refugees.

U.S. aid, which reached massive proportions, serves two essential purposes: to implement the slaughter, and to pay off the elite groups that benefit from it. Some two-thirds of the aid flows directly to the foreign bank accounts of these beneficiaries of the counterinsurgency program, who naturally would much prefer that the U.S. taxpayer finance the operation while enriching them on the side. In effect, the U.S. taxpayer is bribing the wealthy to stay in place while the slaughter continues. Meanwhile the country is sinking into economic decline, less because of the war than because of capital flight.

In this respect, the story is rather typical. The famous Latin American debt, now a topic of major international concern, is roughly comparable in scale to the foreign capital reserves of the Latin American super-rich. Again we see one of the realities of foreign aid: a means by which the poor in the wealthy societies pay the wealthy in the poor societies for their services to the wealthy in the wealthy societies.

The recent history of intervention in El Salvador is one of the more sordid episodes in U.S. history. It was also a substantial success. The popular organizations were largely destroyed. The threat of democracy was stilled. The enthusiastic response of Western elites to this exercise in "fostering democracy" is therefore easy to understand.

Returning again to Kennedy's answer to our question: the U.S. will also favor a Trujillo, or worse, if there is a danger that popular organizations based on the Church, peasant associations, unions, and the like, threaten to lay the basis for meaningful democracy. We learn, once again, that the concept of a "Castro" is quite broad in scope.

Recent events in Nicaragua provide further insight into the official answer to our question. The Somoza dynasty were valued friends, though as in the case of Trujillo, Marcos, Duvalier and other U.S.-backed gangsters, problems arose as Somoza's thuggery extended too broadly, affecting the business classes as well as the normal and proper victims, and as popular opposition to his corruption and violence began to escape control. As long as it seemed that Somoza could hold out, the U.S. supported him, in part directly, in part through the medium of mercenary states that are regularly called upon for such purposes when the U.S. role must be concealed from the public. When it became clear in 1979 that Somoza could no longer be maintained, the Carter Administration made the normal and predictable policy shift, advocating "Somocismo without Somoza," exactly as in other similar cases. The two major concerns were: that the National Guard, trained for many years by the United States and enjoying close contacts with the U.S. military, be maintained in existence to ensure "stability" and "order"; and that business-based elites be in a position to dominate and control the political process-that "democracy" in the sense of U.S. Newspeak be instituted.

In pursuance of these aims, the U.S. followed a dual-track policy. One was the reconstitution of the National Guard, from 1979 according to Nicaraguan exiles and Salvadoran officers who participated, with aid and training from agents of the neo-Nazi Argentine generals acting "as a proxy for the United States in Central America" (terrorism specialist Brian Jenkins of the Rand Corporation) from 1980, and direct U.S. control from 1981. The second track was an early offer of aid to the new government, but designed so as to strengthen the private business sector. U.S. aid was also supported by international banks, which feared that Nicaragua would not be able to service the vast debt resulting from their collaboration with Somoza, particularly now that he had fled with a large part of the country's remaining assets. As usual, aid was to be a device to compel the U.S. taxpayer to subsidize the wealthy and powerful, at home and abroad. This final effort to ensure the continuity of the old regime, to bar unwanted social reforms, and to pay off U.S. banks is regularly described in the U.S. as a demonstration of the remarkable magnanimity of the U.S. government and the bad faith of the Sandinistas, who persisted in their evil ways nevertheless. These evil ways proved serious indeed. The crimes of the Sandinistas were soon demonstrated by remarkable improvements in health, literacy, nutritional levels and social welfare. In January 1983, the Inter-American Development Bank, summarizing developments since 1979, concluded that "Nicaragua has made noteworthy progress in the social sector, which is laying a solid foundation for long-term socio-economic development," including health, literacy, community organizing, food production for the population, and so on. The charitable development agency Oxfam America, in a report on Central America, observed in 1985 that among the countries of the region where Oxfam works (Guatemala, El Salvador, Honduras and Nicaragua), "only in Nicaragua has a substantial effort been made to address inequities in land ownership and to extend health, educational, and agricultural services to poor peasant families," though the contra war—fulfilling its objectives—"has slowed the pace of social reform and compounded hunger in the northern countryside." As I mentioned yesterday, the parent organization of Oxfam in London went still further, declaring Nicaragua to be "exceptional" among the 76 countries where Oxfam has worked in the government's commitment "to improving the condition of the people and encouraging their active participation in the development process"—thus posing what Oxfam accurately terms "the threat of a good example." The World Bank described the dedication of the government to improving the lives of the poor as "remarkable" (June 1983), and identified its projects in Nicaragua as among the best it had supported, noting the absence of corruption and the concern for the poor. Naturally, the U.S. has worked effectively to block further projects of this sort. Particularly offensive are projects that would provide services to private farmers, since these would not only benefit the country economically but would also harm the propaganda image of a totalitarian state carefully crafted by the U.S. ideological system.

These crimes are intolerable for the reasons that I have already discussed. It was necessary to respond in the usual manner: by international terrorism, embargo, pressures on international institutions and allies to withhold aid, a huge campaign of propaganda and disinformation, threatening military maneuvers and overflights as part of what the Administration calls "perception management," and other hostile measures available to a powerful and violent state. Near hysteria was evoked in the U.S. government when Nicaragua accepted the draft of the Contadora treaty in 1984, shortly after Ronald Reagan had informed Congress that the purpose of the contra war was to compel Nicaragua to accept the treaty and Secretary of State Shultz had praised the draft treaty and denounced Nicaragua for blocking its implementation. Hysteria reached a still higher peak when Nicaragua conducted elections described by the professional association of U.S. Latin America scholars (LASA) as remarkably open and honest despite massive U.S. efforts to undermine them, including pressures on the business-based opposition and a disinformation campaign about the delivery of MIG aircraft, carefully timed to remove the elections from the news; it is, of course, taken for granted across the political spectrum that if Nicaragua were to obtain aircraft to defend its national territory from a U.S. assault, that would be an intolerable offense, justifying bombing of Nicaragua, as Senatorial doves warned. The judgment expressed by the LASA observers in their detailed report was shared by almost all international observers; these facts were virtually suppressed in the United States, where the 1984 elections did not take place, according to the government-media consensus. The reaction of the United States to the elections in Nicaragua once again reveals the deep-seated fear and hatred of democratic forms among U.S. elites, if the results cannot be controlled in such as way as to ensure dominance over the social, economic and political system on the part of the business-military alliance linked to U.S. power.

As I mentioned yesterday, Administration officials privately concede that "they are content to see the contras debilitate the Sandinistas by forcing them to divert scarce resources toward the war and away from social programs," a fact that elicits no comment in the U.S. Similarly, there is no reaction when former CIA analyst David MacMichael, testifying at the World Court hearings, describes on the basis of his personal experience the thinking that lay behind the high-level planning to weaken and destabilize the Nicaraguan government:

> . . .the principal actions to be undertaken were paramilitary which hopefully would provoke cross-border attacks by Nicaraguan forces and thus serve to demonstrate Nicaragua's aggressive nature and possibly call into play the Organization of American States' provisions. It was hoped that the Nicaraguan Government would clampdown on civil liberties within Nicaragua itself, arresting its opposition, demonstrating its allegedly inherent totalitarian nature and thus increase domestic dissent within the country.

Elite opinion across the political spectrum in the United States insists that Nicaragua must be "contained" and "isolated," prevented from "exporting its revolution." If possible, the "cancer"—as Ronald Reagan, George Shultz and others call it—must be eradicated, though there are differences in tactical judgments as to how this necessary task should be accomplished. As in other cases already discussed, the "rotten apple theory" has two versions. For the public, the danger is that Nicaragua, a Soviet client and military base, will conquer the Hemisphere and take all we have. The real concern is over the "demonstration effect" of successful development in terms that might be meaningful to suffering people elsewhere, endangering the Fifth Freedom as the "virus" causes "contagion" and "the rot spreads." The utter absurdity of the public charges, and the astonishing series of lies and deception in which they are couched, suffice to establish the conclusion that the U.S. is following its conventional course of action in this case.

The lies and deception are in fact remarkable. A revealing example is the State Department document *Revolution Beyond Our Borders* published in September 1985 in an obvious effort to counter the (minimal) possibility that the concurrent World Court proceedings might evoke a spark of interest here. As I mentioned earlier, the title is based on a mistranslation of a speech by Tomás Borge in which he explains that Nicaragua cannot "export our revolution" but can only "export our example," while "the people themselves of these countries . . . must make their revolutions." The State Department effort to distort these comments into a proof of aggressive intent was exposed immediately by the Council on Hemispheric Affairs, and is surely known to the media; it is, in fact, only one incident in a series of similar lies, all exposed in due course. But the story continues. In his June 1986 speech that induced the House to support contra aid, after warning of the threat to our existence posed by Nicaragua, the Great Communicator worked his way to the final climactic flourish: "Communist Nicaragua," he declaimed, is "dedicated—in the words of its own leaders—to a 'revolution without borders'." In short, they themselves admit that they intend to conquer and destroy us.

The media response was instructive. Reagan's invocation of this dramatic Communist admission of their aggressive intent was reported without comment in the *New York Times* and elsewhere, though—it must be stressed again—the facts were well-known to any journalist of minimal competence. In an interview with Nicaraguan Vice-President Sergio Ramírez, the *Washington Post* challenged him to explain away the statement by Tomás Borge in July 1981 that "This revolution goes beyond the borders," the alleged source of Reagan's charge. At the dovish extreme of the U.S. media, the editors of the *Boston Globe* wrote that "the State Department has never been able to document any arms shipment to back up the Sandinistas' boast about 'a revolution without borders'," adding that "their failure to spread their revolution, and their humiliating silence about it, should be taken as a sign of reassurance, but is ignored in Washington." "Conservative" commentators naturally exulted in the episode. The President's advisers could have perfect confidence that the media would not expose the fraud, continuing to fulfill their function at a critical moment, as they did, another magnificent testimonial to the glories of the Free Press.

Particularly noteworthy is the reaction of the doves. They oppose contra aid on the basis of the "humiliating silence" of the Sandinistas over their failure to back up their "boast" that the success of their revolution would inspire others. The doves feel no need to explain that the President was lying about the "boast" and that the real "boast" failed thanks to U.S.-inspired international terrorism. And most instructive of all, they find it "reassuring" that the Sandinistas' efforts "to address inequities in land ownership and to extend health, educational, and agricultural services to poor peasant families," unique among 76 developing countries (Oxfam), have failed thanks to U.S. violence. One sees here, brilliantly exhibited, the genius of the incomparable U.S. system of indoctrination, with doves and hawks competing to determine who can be more abject in their service to state deception and violence.

In the past years, the Sandinistas have been accused of everything from drug-trafficking to genocide, while the unquestioned facts about their social and economic programs are close to unmentionable within the major media and journals. Take one typical and important example, the first three months of 1986, when attention was focused on the impending Congressional votes on contra aid. During this period, the *New York Times* and *Washington Post* ran 85 pieces by columnists and invited contributors. Opinions on the Sandinistas ran from harshly critical (virtually all) to critical but more conditionally so; thus 100 percent uniformity was maintained on the central issue. Alleged apologists for the Sandinistas were bitterly denounced (anonymously, to assure no possibility of response), but none were allowed a voice, though sympathetic voices could have been found even within the ideological constraints of the media. It is particularly impressive that the two most striking features of the Sandinista regime were almost entirely ignored amidst a chorus of abuse: the constructive social programs, and the fact that in sharp contrast to U.S. clients such as Duarte in El Salvador, the government has not engaged in large-scale torture and slaughter. The latter point is nowhere mentioned, reflecting a general tendency to dismiss atrocities in our domains as defects of little significance. As for the first point, apart from an oblique reference by Abraham Brumberg (former director of the State Department journal *Problems of Communism,* who has given nuanced and, in my view, quite plausible assessments of the Sandinista government elsewhere), there is only one phrase referring to the Sandinista programs in the areas of health, literacy, land reform and development: by Tad Sculz (*NYT,* March 16), in the course of a denunciation of the "generally appalling leadership" in this "repressive society" and "its failures." These programs are crucial to understanding the U.S. attack against Nicaragua, as we have seen; correspondingly, no mention of the basic reasons for the U.S. war was permitted in these opinion columns. Exactly the same is true of editorial opinion. In 80 *New York Times* editorials on Nicaragua from 1980 through mid-1986, I found two phrases on these crucial features of the Sandinista government.

There was, of course, debate in the 85 opinion columns: over the proper way for the United States to respond to Sandinista abuses and crimes. One will search in vain for a debate over whether we should establish a terrorist army to attack El Salvador, where the crimes are vastly worse, or the United States, with its long history of encouragement and support for hideous atrocities in the region. This sharply limited debate helps maintain the impression that we live in an "open society," but as in the case of Indochina and much else, it is important to ensure that the debate proceeds within the framework established by the centers of power so that its presuppositions are established as the bounds of thinkable thought.

The techniques employed to efface the record and to demonstrate Sandinista "failures" are illuminating, and serve again to illustrate the seriousness of the underlying concerns that are being concealed. Thus, the Presidential Kissinger Commission sought to demonstrate that Sandinista "mismanagement" was responsible for an economic decline during a period of economic growth by taking 1977 as the base-line. This "clever sophistry," as historian Thomas Walker describes it, allowed them to attribute the collapse of the economy during the U.S.-backed Somoza repression and massacre of 1978-9 to the Sandinistas, and to suppress the early recovery from the carnage. In the real world, the economy collapsed from 1977 to 1979 while the U.S. and its Israeli client continued to back the Somoza regime through its final outburst of violence, and then recovered rapidly until the contra war aborted this dangerous development. Through 1984, despite the contra war and the "capital strike," the per capita growth rate in Nicaragua was superior to that of any other Central American country, while per capita consumption of most basic goods increased. Selection of 1977 as a base-line is a convenient device to obscure the early improvements that caused such profound concern in Washington.

The same device is used by cynical Western intellectuals in Europe as well. The respected sociologist Ralf Dahrendorf explains that the economy "had begun to decline in 1977" while "after the revolution, decline became a plunge," with per capita GNP halved "between 1977 and 1985" and no "significant redistribution of income," a proof of Sandinista failures. He also tells us with utter confidence what "most Nicaraguans believe," after having spent a few days in Nicaragua with a visiting delegation.

Such pronouncements on the part of visiting dignitaries a re incidentally quite standard, and are considered entirely proper as long as the figure in question maintains doctrinal purity, as determined in Washington. Thus Robert Leiken, a leading contra lobbyist and media favorite, assures his Western audience with equal confidence, on the basis of his no less profound inquiries, that support for the Sandinistas has "virtually vanished" while the contras have "broad support in the Nicaraguan countryside and the quiet sympathies of many urban Nicaraguans."

The elaborate array of hysterical lies and deception has reached proportions so astonishing as to elicit some comment even in the Establishment media. Deceit on this scale is an important and revealing phenomenon. The flood of lies plainly conceals some simple truths. The first of these is that the United States is devoting itself with desperate intensity to drive Nicaragua into the hands of the Soviet Union, so as to justify the U.S. attack against Nicaragua in "self-defense." The second of these simple truths is the real reason for the attack, concealed in the flood of lies: namely, the reason I have already discussed, the threat of a good example, which must be extirpated before the "virus" spreads, "infecting" the region and beyond. These truths are evident from the actual record in the present case and are fully in accord with traditional U.S. practice that is completely rational in terms of the real interests that determine policy. In accordance with the same operative principles and practice, these truths are also inexpressible within the U.S. ideological system, and with rare exceptions, among U.S. allies as well.

The case of Nicaragua supplements still further our understanding of Kennedy's official answer to our question. The U.S. will prefer "a Trujillo" whenever "the threat of a good example" arises in its domains. Those who devote themselves to the needs of the poor majority, or who seek to construct a political system that will not be controlled by business-based groups and a military system not linked to and dominated by the United States, are "Castros" who must be driven to reliance on the Soviet Union by unremitting attack, subjected to terrorist violence and other pressures, and crucially, prevented from perpetrating the crime of successful development in the interest of the poor majority.

These are the real reasons for the attack on Nicaragua. The official reasons barely merit contempt and I will waste no time here refuting them.

I often address these questions in the United States and Europe, not, of course, in the major media (though Europe, in this regard, is still quite different and far more open), but before audiences to which access cannot be prevented by the state and the private ideological institutions—an important matter, to which I will return in the last lecture. I generally conclude with some remarks on our responsibilities and how we should pursue them. Some of us here are from the Western industrial democracies and Costa Rica, countries where fear of state violence need not impede active protest against the policies that maintain "stability" and "order," though the distribution of effective power over the social, political and economic system and the media renders these tasks difficult and often frustrating. Most of you live here, and I would not presume to give you advice, apart from one brief word.

It is useful and instructive to pay heed to Reaganite fanaticism. Properly interpreted, it contains very sound advice. Listen to what the state terrorists say, and undertake to do the opposite. Their fondest wish is that Nicaragua should become what they describe it to be: a Soviet client, a brutally repressive and totalitarian state "at war with God and man" in their terms, holding its terrified population under control with the whip and the bludgeon. Their greatest fear is that Nicaragua should pursue "the logic of the majority," with dedicated efforts to devote its meager resources to the needs of the poor and deprived, and with freedom and genuine popular participation. U.S. savagery is designed to realize the hope and to eliminate the fear. Those who oppose these contemptible policies will work to frustrate the hope and to bring the fears to fruition.

LECTURE 4

National Security Policy

So far, I have been discussing various aspects of U.S. foreign policy, its plans and principles and their execution in practice. In this lecture, I would like to turn to a different though related matter: national security policy, the arms race, and the threat of nuclear war.

The first point that must be stressed, though it should be obvious, is that the situation is quite serious. There is a danger of terminal nuclear war. How great this danger is, no one can say with any precision. But the probability of catastrophe is surely well beyond what any rational person should accept with equanimity.

The use of nuclear weapons has been considered numerous times in the past, and in some of these cases, the steps that were taken carried substantial risk. A Brookings Institution study by Barry Blechman and Stephen Kaplan, based on recently released records of the Strategic Air Command, documents 19 cases between 1946 and 1973 when the U.S. deployed strategic nuclear weapons or placed them on alert, ready for use. The frequency of these occasions indicates that the national leadership has always regarded the use of nuclear weapons as a live policy option. There have been other cases when the use of such weapons was considered and even threatened, or when international tensions brought the superpowers close to a confrontation that might have led to their use. As for tactical nuclear weapons, we may

117

usefully recall the discussion by General Nathan Twining, Chairman of the Joint Chiefs of Staff under President Eisenhower. Writing in the mid-1960s, he explained that these weapons, "if employed once or twice on the right targets, at the right time, would in my judgment, stop *current* aggression, and stop *future* subversion and limited wars before they start" (his emphasis). By "current aggression," he was plainly referring to the "internal aggression" of the Vietnamese against the American invaders and their client armies. He gave several examples to illustrate what he meant by "subversion": Cuba, the Congo, and Vietnam, three countries where subversion had indeed been rife, including attempts to assassinate the political leadership (as occurred in the Congo and Vietnam)—namely, subversion by the United States. The idea that it would be appropriate to use nuclear weapons "to stop future subversion" is noteworthy, and departs from the norm (at least what is publicly expressed), though General Twining's concept of "subversion" and "aggression" is quite standard. Recall that under the Orwellian principles of Western logic, it is a matter of definition, not of fact, that the United States is never the agent of subversion or aggression; hence by simple logic, enemies of the United States must be guilty of subversion and aggression in their own countries if they act in ways displeasing to the Master and come into conflict with his designs.

One might, incidentally, imagine the reaction in the West if some top Soviet military commander, or Moammar Qaddafi or Khomeini, were to issue such pronouncements about the use of nuclear weapons.

Some of the 19 incidents when U.S. strategic nuclear forces were involved might surprise you. At least, they surprised me when I learned about them. One such occasion, for example, was an election in Uruguay in 1947. Another was the CIA coup in Guatemala in 1954. As part of the background planning, the U.S. dispatched nuclear-armed bombers to Nicaragua, "meant, it would appear, as a signal of American commitment," Blech-man and Kaplan observe. We see that the need to destroy Guatemalan democracy was taken very seriously. Recall that this took place before things went sour in Nicaragua. These were "the good old days," when the country was still available as a base for U.S. terrorism, subversion and aggression and there was therefore no need for Western humanists to agonize over democracy and human rights in Nicaragua or to conduct a terrorist war in order "to fit Nicaragua back into a Central American mode" and to "demand reasonable conduct by a regional standard," the proper goal of U.S. policy, the editors of the *Washington Post* declare—the "regional standard" and "Central American mode" being exemplified by El Salvador, Guatemala, Honduras, and the Somoza regime.

The most famous of the 19 incidents was the Cuban missile crisis, when U.S. planners estimated the probability of war at one-third to one-half as they rejected Khrushchev's offer to end the crisis by the simultaneous withdrawal of Soviet missiles from Cuba and American missiles from Turkey—obsolete missiles in the latter case (they were being replaced by Polaris submarines), for which a withdrawal order had already been issued but not yet executed. This remarkable decision is regarded with much pride among U.S. elites. The major study of the crisis, by Harvard Professor Graham Allison, describes the handling of the crisis as "one of the finest examples of diplomatic prudence, and perhaps the finest hour of John F. Kennedy's Presidency," while noting that "had war come, it would have meant the death of 100 million Americans, more than 100 million Russians, as well as millions of Europeans." This reaction to what surely must count as one of the lowest points of human history-a reaction quite widely shared—merits no little concern among rational people.

Turkey remains today a major U.S. nuclear outpost, with nuclear-armed aircraft constantly on "alert" status, aimed at the

Soviet Union. Turkey is also part of the base structure ringing the
Middle East oil-producing regions, "a stupendous source of strategic power and one of the greatest material prizes in world history,"
as the State Department described it in 1945. One major function
of the U.S. strategic nuclear forces in Turkey, as elsewhere, is to
deter what would be called "Soviet aggression": namely, a Soviet
response should the U.S. choose to dispatch military forces to this
region to "defend" it against "internal aggression."

The Central America-Caribbean region remains a possible
point of conflict that might lead to nuclear confrontation. Sup-
pose that the U.S. proxy army attacking Nicaragua does not
prove adequate to its assigned tasks: to carry out sufficient terror
and destruction to impede social reforms, and to "increase domestic dissent within the country" and compel the government
to demonstrate "its allegedly inherent totalitarian nature" by
clamping down on civil liberties, one goal of the U.S. operations
according to David MacMichael's World Court testimony, which
I quoted in the last lecture. If the contra armies fail to achieve
these worthy goals, the U.S. might turn to other means. One
possibility, as MacMichael has suggested elsewhere, would be to
try to block shipping to Nicaragua, perhaps with the same high-
speed Piranha naval craft that were used in earlier CIA terrorist
operations. Proposals to this effect have already been advanced,
in particular, by Senator Dave Omenberger, chairman of the Sen-
ate Select Committee on Intelligence. Nicaragua does not have
the means to react, but Cuba and the Soviet Union do. The assumption of U.S. planners would be that as in the past, the Soviet Union would back away from a dangerous confrontation
likely to lead to nuclear war. If they do, a blockade will have been
instituted, and the hope would be that Nicaragua would soon be
defenseless against attack while the population would be unable
or unwilling to accept the inevitable privation and suffering resulting from an effective blockade.

If the USSR and Cuba were to respond to these acts of violence, there would be a hysterical outcry in the United States, orchestrated by the state propaganda apparatus with the participation of the mass media, in the usual and familiar fashion. Secretary of the Navy John Lehman has predicted that any U.S. attempt to blockade Nicaragua might trigger a U.S.-Soviet naval conflict, which would be "instantaneously a global war." That any such confrontation could be limited is hardly likely; it might well spell the end of human history.

Again, no one can offer a realistic estimate of the likelihood of such a sequence of events. It is, in fact, likely that the Soviet Union would be unwilling to face the risks. But no one can be sure, and confrontations may easily get out of hand in unpredictable ways.

For the past 20 years, by far the greatest danger has been in the Middle East, an area of vast strategic importance because of its unparalleled energy resources, largely controlled by the U.S. since it succeeded in displacing France and Britain during and after World War II. The U.S. would surely not tolerate any Soviet move that might threaten its domination of the major oil-producing regions. The level of armaments within the region is phenomenal, the superpowers are present in force on the periphery, and the region is torn by many serious conflicts. Among them, the most threatening for world peace is the long-lasting Arab-Israeli conflict.

Since the early 1960s, Israel has increasingly been perceived as a "strategic asset" by U.S. planners, serving as a barrier to "radical Arab nationalism" (to translate from Newspeak: nationalist movements that do not follow U.S. orders, as distinct from "moderate" elements that understand their place). The 1967 Arab-Israeli war solidified this relationship, as Israel crushed the "radical nationalist" threat of Nasser, and subsequent developments have extended it more fully. Correspondingly, the U.S. has

blocked the possibility—very real, in the past 15 years—of a political settlement in accordance with a very broad international
consensus with guarantees for the security and territorial integrity of all stares in the region, including Israel and a new Pales-
tinian state in the occupied West Bank and Gaza Strip. As long
as the military confrontation persists, Israel will be utterly dependent on the United States, hence dependable, a highly mili-
tarized, technologically advanced state serving U.S. strategic
interests as a Middle East gendarme and available for service as
a "mercenary state" to carry our U.S. missions, as in Central
America during the past decade.

This persistent regional military confrontation, which regularly explodes into war and probably will again, carries constant
risks of superpower confrontation as well. In 1983, Robert Mc-
Namara commented that "we damn near had war" in June 1967
when the U.S. "turned around a [Soviet] carrier in the Mediterranean" during the Arab-Israel war; at the time, McNamara was
Defense Secretary in the Johnson Administration. He did not
give further details, but the incident probably took place during
Israel's conquest of the Syrian Golan Heights after the cease-
fire, an act that elicited severe warnings from the USSR. The Soviet and U.S. fleets were present in force in the Eastern
Mediterranean. There were also several "hot line" communications during the war, apparently of a fairly threatening nature;
according to McNamara, at one point Soviet Premier Kosygin
warned Johnson over the hot line that "if you want war, you'll
have war." In 1973, the U.S. called a strategic nuclear alert in response to a Soviet warning to Israel when Israeli forces were attempting to destroy the encircled Egyptian Third Army after the
cease-fire and with the Israeli army in a position to shell Damas-
cus. During Israel's invasion of Lebanon in 1982, supported by
the U.S. throughout, the Soviet and U.S. fleets again approached
direct confrontation and there were warnings of a Soviet re-

sponse if Israel escalated its attack against Syria, a Russian ally. Tensions continued as the U.S. landed Marines in Lebanon in an attempt to secure the Israeli-imposed government after the Lebanese resistance had compelled Israel to withdraw from most of the territory it had conquered. A Syrian-Israeli war is not unlikely; many military experts in Israel regard it as virtually inevitable, with only the timing in doubt. If this occurs, there is again a very serious danger that it will involve the superpowers, leading to direct confrontation and probable nuclear war.

These examples illustrate what is surely the greatest threat of nuclear war. Contrary to what is commonly alleged, there is little threat of a war breaking out over European issues or a Soviet drive towards the Persian Gulf—the fantasy of the early 1980s. Nor has any of this ever been very likely apart from several conflicts over the status of Berlin in earlier years, though Europe might well be drawn into a war erupting over tensions elsewhere. The primary danger of nuclear war derives from what is sometimes called "the deadly connection," that is, the possibility that some Third World conflict will escalate out of control, engaging the superpowers. The greatest danger by far is in the Middle East, since the mid-1960s, but the threat is not small elsewhere, including Central America. In these and other regions, U.S. policy is a major factor, though not the only one, in stimulating and maintaining tensions and conflicts that might lead to nuclear war.

The threat of a nuclear war is severe, but the issues that are the focus of most discussion are of little significance and the debate itself is often seriously misleading. The major issues currently discussed are the scale of strategic weapons deployed and Reagan's "Star Wars" (SDI; Strategic Defense Initiative). As for the first, it is commonly observed that the number of war heads and missiles deployed by the superpowers is so enormous and their destructive force is so great that each could destroy the other—and most of the world with them—many times over. But even if missiles and warheads were reduced to some small fraction of the existing arsenals, the consequences of a nuclear exchange would be intolerably grave, and there is no obvious relation between the size of nuclear arsenals and the likelihood of their use.

As for Star Wars, most current debate centers on whether such a system can work: the doves argue that it cannot and the hawks counter that it might. But in fact, the system is much more dangerous to the extent that it seems likely to work. Of course, it will never defend any country against a first strike; only fanatics can believe any such fantasy. But it is conceivable that it might limit the damage from a retaliatory strike and thus undermine the deterrent of the adversary (though even that is unlikely; even without expert knowledge, one can be fairly confident that extremely complex technology which, in the nature of the case, cannot be fully tested, will malfunction). The adversary must make a "worst case" analysis, assuming that the system might work and planning accordingly. In times of crisis, with no time for deliberation, the worst case analysis might motivate a first strike in desperation, the retaliatory capacity having been challenged. That is exactly how the U.S. would respond if the Soviet Union were capable of deploying a defensive shield of even limited capacity, and there is no reason to doubt that Soviet planners will reason the same way. The development of such "defensive" systems thus substantially increases the likelihood of resort to nuclear weapons in times of crisis—and furthermore, the components of SDI are by no means solely "defensive weapons."

Apart from "the deadly connection," the primary threat of nuclear war lies in the constant technical advances in weaponry: the development of highly accurate, very destructive and perhaps undetectable offensive weapons, and allegedly defensive systems such as SDI. Such systems as these drive the adversary to adopt exceedingly dangerous countermeasures, such as computerized response strategies and pre-delegation of authority to lower level officers. Highly accurate missiles with a short flight time reduce the opportunity for human intervention while threatening loss of the deterrent and "decapitation" of the high command. Thus they compel reliance on computer-controlled "launch-on-warning" strategies and on junior officers. Even now, U.S. submarine commanders have substantial authority to launch a nuclear strike, a matter recently discussed by Desmond Ball in the journal *International Security*. The same is true of Reagan's SDI, which also enhances the likelihood of a first strike in desperation, for the reasons just mentioned.

We know that U.S. computerized systems have frequently malfunctioned; there have been numerous occasions when a technical error or misinterpretation of incoming data called for a programmed nuclear strike that was aborted by human intervention. The Soviet systems are surely far more inefficient and will fail far more often. By compelling the Soviet Union to increase its reliance on such systems, the U.S. is therefore severely endangering its security, and the possibility of human survival.

The major weapons systems currently being deployed by the U.S. have exactly this effect. Trident submarine-launched missiles, which are highly accurate, fast, and very destructive, threaten the land-based deterrent on which the Soviet Union relies. These weapons therefore drive the Soviet Union to adopt countermeasures that are extremely threatening to U.S. security, exactly as in the case of Reagan's SDI. The weapons systems currently under development and deployment by the U.S. threaten the security of the United States, increasing the likelihood of its destruction if only by inadvertence, error or miscalculation in times of crisis. Furthermore, sooner or later the USSR will duplicate this military technology, thus forcing the U.S. to the same mad reliance on computerized response systems that are guaranteed to fail and on predelegation of authority with its enormous risks. The same process will lead U.S. planner to "worst case analyses" that will increase the likelihood of a first strike in times of crisis.

To summarize, there are serious threats of war, but they do not lie primarily in the domain of most of the current debate between hawks and doves. The hawks warn of the prospect of a Soviet attack on Western Europe or a drive on the Persian Gulf, highly remote eventualities except in the context of conflict arising over other issues. The doves deplore the size of nuclear arsenals and the incapacity of Star Wars to meet its proclaimed goals; the former is not the core of the problem, and the latter concern is misplaced, as noted. The real problems lie elsewhere. Primary among them are Third World intervention which establishes the "deadly connection" and the steady technical progress in weapons design. In both respects, U.S. policies enhance the threat of nuclear war and the likelihood of its own destruction, by virtue of its leading role in maintaining and enhancing Third World tensions that might explode into superpower confrontation, and in development of more advanced weaponry. Furthermore, these issues are of little concern to planners, and are only marginal to current debate. The U.S. is committed to Third World intervention and technical advances in weaponry despite the serious threat posed to U.S. security.

These considerations lift the curtain on a dirty little secret: security is at most a marginal concern of security planners.

A look at strategic planning suggests similar conclusions. Strategic analysts often observe that planning appears to be highly irrational. Take the case of SDI, once again. Whatever slight prospects such a system might offer for defense of the national territory depend crucially on general reduction of offensive forces, to prevent the adversary from over whelming the system with new offensive weapons. But other current U.S. programs, such as the Trident D-5 missiles, guarantee that the USSR will follow suit, increasing its offensive capacity, and the generally

evasive U.S. attitude towards arms control has the same consequences. Furthermore, a Ballistic Missile Defense (BMD) system such as SDI requires that the adversary cooperate by not
deploying weapons that will by pass the system, cruise missiles
for example. While the Reagan Administration is charging ahead
with SDI, it is deploying hundreds of sea-launched cruise missiles
(SLCMs) instead of responding to Soviet offers to bar such
weapons. Hence the Soviet Union will surely do exactly the same
thing, a few years down the road. As a number of analysts have
commented, "if unconstrained by arms control, these Soviet
SLCMs will provide an excellent counter to a U.S. BMD system,
no matter how effective such a system is against Soviet ballistic
missiles. Indeed, the Soviets have a distinct geographical advantage in deploying SLCMs, because of our country's long coast-
lines and the fact that the majority of our population lives a long
these coasts. A BMD system and other types of strategic defenses cannot hope to begin reducing the nuclear threat unless
constraints are placed on the production and deployment of
SLCMs and other types of cruise missiles, despite the verification problems such constraints will pose for arms control" (Jeffrey Boutwell and F. A. Long).

The evident irrationality of these programs, as measured by
effects upon security, suggests that security is not a driving motive, whatever tortured explanations may be offered.

Why is every U.S. Administration so committed to this race
towards destruction? There is a conventional answer: it is necessary to defend ourselves against the Evil Empire that is committed
to our destruction, "the monolithic and ruthless conspiracy" to
take over the world, to use John F. Kennedy's phrase. But this conventional answer conveys very little information, because it is entirely predictable, whatever the facts. The aggressive and militant
actions of every state are invariably justified on grounds of "defense." Thus Hitler's aggression in Eastern Europe was justified as

defense against "a dagger pointed at the heart of Germany" (Czechoslovakia), against the violence and aggressiveness of the Poles, against the encirclement of the imperialist powers that sought to strangle Germany; and his invasion of the Low Countries and France was also "defensive," a response to the hostile acts of France and England, bent on Germany's destruction. If we had records, we would probably discover that Attila the Hun was acting in self-defense. Since state actions are always justified in terms of defense, we learn nothing when we hear that certain specific actions are so justified except that we are listening to the spokesperson for some state; but that we already knew.

To evaluate the defensive rhetoric, it is necessary to investigate the historical circumstances and record. When we do, we generally find little merit in the claims, and the present case is no exception. Current U.S. international and security policy severely threaten the security of the United States. It is not the first time.

Consider the situation in 1950, when the first great postwar increase in the military system began, with the military budget tripled. The conventional explanation is that this was a reaction to the Korean War, which was interpreted as proof of Moscow's intent to take over the world. The explanation is hardly credible. For one thing, the proposal to undertake a vast expansion of the military system as part of a "rollback strategy" against the Soviet Union was proposed in NSC-68 several months prior to the Korean War, as I mentioned in the first lecture. Hence it could hardly have been a reaction to Soviet aggression in Korea. Furthermore, there was no evidence then, nor is there now, that the North Korean invasion was a Soviet initiative; rather, U.S. planners seized upon the invasion as a way of justifying the plans laid out in NSC-68, to which they were committed for quite different reasons. And as I discussed earlier, what we call "the Korean War" was only a phase in a much longer conflict, which began when the U.S. destroyed the indigenous national movement in Korea in the late 1940s with considerable brutality, also blocking the unification of Korea that was widely advocated by Korean nationalists in the South as well as the Northern half of the country. In fact, border incidents were frequent in the late 1940s, the majority of them southern-initiated. All in all, it is impossible to take the defensive rhetoric seriously in this case.

Furthermore, consider the general state of U.S. security in 1950. As I've discussed in earlier lectures, the U.S. emerged from World War II in a position of power with few if any historical precedents, possessing about 50% of the world 's wealth and utterly secure from attack. It had no enemies in the Western Hemisphere, and controlled both oceans and large areas beyond. There was, in fact, one potential threat to U.S. security, as yet unrealized: the development of Intercontinental Ballistic Missiles (ICBMs) with highly destructive (hydrogen bomb) warheads. A concern for security would have plainly dictated efforts to prevent the development of such weapons systems, the only ones that could seriously threaten the United States. The record shows no such efforts, though it might well have been possible to bar development and deployment of such weapons. It was not until the 1970s that the USSR had a significant ICBM capacity, leaving ample time for negotiations on the matter, never undertaken or, as far as we know, seriously contemplated by U.S. planners. The analogue to the current case of SLCMs, Trident missiles, SDI and other military systems that threaten U.S. security is evident. Again, it seems that security was a matter of marginal concern to U.S. planners.

The first major expansion of the U.S. military system was undertaken in the early 1950s, but not for reasons of security and not for protection of European and other allies, as we have already discussed. The same is true of the next significant expansion under the Kennedy Administration, which set off the current phase of the arms race with the deployment of 1000 Minutemen missiles and other programs, including a substantial investment in counterinsurgency (meaning, international terrorism) as well as the crucial change in the mission of the Latin American military, with its dire consequences, which I mentioned in the last lecture. In this case, the official excuse was the "missile gap." During the 1960 presidential campaign, the Kennedy liberals denounced Eisenhower in much the same terms used by the Reaganites against Jimmy Carter in the 1980 campaign. Eisenhower was weak and indecisive. He was frittering away our wealth in luxuries while the Russians marched from strength to strength, threatening to develop a commanding lead in missiles that would enable them to destroy us and to conquer the world. Eisenhower responded that there was no "missile gap," and he was right. The "missile gap" was as much a fraud as the "bomber gap" that preceded it. In fact, there was a missile gap, but it was in favor of the U.S., by about 10 to 1; the Russians had *four* operational missiles at the time, and these were exposed and could easily have been destroyed.

The Kennedy Administration quickly discovered that there was no "missile gap" in favor of the USSR, if its strategists did not know this all along, but considered this fact of no significance. In an internal memo, National Security adviser McGeorge Bundy wrote that the phrase "missile gap" had had a "useful shorthand effect of calling attention to. . .our basic military posture," that is, escalation of the arms race and expansion of intervention capacity. Therefore the arms build-up must continue, quite apart from the clearly fraudulent excuse. Again, security was not the issue.

Much the same is true of the current military build-up, the most rapid and extreme peacetime military expansion in U.S. history. The plans for expansion of the military system and a cutback in social programs were laid by the Carter Administration prior to the Iranian hostage crisis and the Soviet invasion of Afghanistan, which provided a pretext to put them into effect. These policies were then significantly expanded under Reagan—though his military budget largely follows the projections of the Carter Administration—under the pretext of a "window of vulnerability" which was as fraudulent as the "missile gap," as is now conceded on all sides, even by Administration spokesmen. The arms build-up has been accompanied by an unending series of fabrications about alleged Soviet military superiority and threats to our existence. As in other cases I have discussed, the fraud conceals the true reasons for the military build-up and the general expansion of the state system under Reagan of which it is one central component. Whatever these reasons are, questions of security from armed attack for the U.S. or its allies are plainly not prominent among them.

Further evidence that security is at most a marginal issue is provided by the current U.S. reaction to Gorbachev's proposals for détente. These proposals include a unilateral ban on nuclear weapons tests, initiated by the USSR for six months in August 1985 and renewed again this year; a proposal for simultaneous abolition of the Warsaw Pact and the NATO military alliance; a proposal to remove the Soviet and U.S. fleets from the Mediterranean (steps that would sharply reduce the threat of the "deadly connection" arising from the Middle East conflicts); and others. These proposals have been dismissed or simply ignored in the United States, again, with substantial deceit, echoed by the subservient media. In the case of the test ban, for example, the Reagan Administration reacted with the claim that it was meaningless because the USSR had just completed an accelerated test series. This claim, loyally reiterated by the national press, was sheer deception. The USSR had carried out fewer tests than in the preceding year, fewer tests in 1985 than the U.S. and far fewer overall. Bur Gorbachev's initiative was dismissed, along with a se-

ries of other ones which, if pursued, might have led to a significant
reduction in international tensions and hence a reduction in
threats to the security and even the existence of the United States.

The case of the test ban is a particularly interesting one. The
Administration argues that a ban on nuclear testing would erode
confidence in weapons, and hence is unacceptable. The doves respond that confidence in these weapons can be retained by testing that does not involve explosion of these devices. If the
Administration position is correct, then a test ban would be highly
beneficial to U.S. security, and in fact, would be a step towards
the alleged goal of SDI: to safeguard the U.S. from a Soviet first
strike. A power that hazards a first strike must have enormous
confidence in its weapons systems (unless the action is taken in
desperation or without human intervention, under conditions of
the sort I discussed in connection with the consequences of the
current U.S. military posture). The first-strike weapons must work
near perfectly, or the enemy will respond with a devastating retaliatory strike. (In fact, this is all in the realm of fantasy, but let
us proceed with the argument nevertheless.) If a test ban would
erode confidence in weapons, it would lessen the probability of a
first strike against the U.S., and hence would increase U.S. security. But this erosion of confidence would not affect the deterrent,
which does not require anything approaching flawless operation.
If a fraction of available nuclear weapons reached their targets,
the result would be an overwhelming catastrophe. Thus if the Administration is correct in its claims, it should strongly favor a test
ban, for these reasons alone.

In fact, a comprehensive ban on testing of nuclear weapons
combined with a ban on missile testing would very likely erode
confidence in weapons, a fact basically agreed on all sides, thus
reducing the possibility of a first strike while retaining the deterrent. It would thus be a safe, costless, verifiable and effective alternative to Star Wars (or more accurately, the alleged purposes

of Star Wars). But the Reagan Administration has no interest in these proposals, nor do the political opposition or the media, apart from fairly marginal elements. These are not live policy options within the political system. Again we must conclude that considerations of security are barely operative, if at all, in the world of national security planning.

The test ban illustrates another crucial fact: the near irrelevance of public opinion. The public supports a nuclear test ban by about 3 to 1, and a majority of the public has indicated support for a unilateral U.S. test ban. I know of no polls that ask whether the U.S. should join the unilateral Soviet test ban, and in fact, it is likely that only a small fraction of the public even knows that it exists, so effectively have they been shielded by the media since it was inaugurated in August 1985. A test ban appears to be feasible, since it is supported by the USSR and, overwhelmingly, by world opinion, as shown continually at the United Nations, where the U.S. has been in a small minority or completely alone in opposing such a step. Highly qualified specialists have testified that there is no serious problem of verification. Thus a comprehensive test ban (particularly, if combined with a ban on testing of missiles) is a policy that is feasible, overwhelmingly supported by world and even domestic opinion, and highly beneficial to U.S. security. But it is not a policy option. In the 1984 elections, for example, the Democrats did not press the issue apart from a few rhetorical flourishes, despite the support for a ban by 75% of the population, an extremely high figure, particularly in the light of the very limited support for this proposal in the media. And if anything, the prospect is even more remote from the political scene today than it was then, despite the dramatic Soviet moves, largely suppressed by the ideological institutions in the United States.

This brief review suggests some interesting conclusions. It seems clear enough that security considerations are of little concern to national security planning, and that public opinion is as irrelevant as the feasibility of measures that would enhance the safety and security of the United States. Plainly, serious concerns, concealed in conventional rhetoric, must be driving the race to destruction.

There are indeed serious concerns, and they are sometimes expressed, even in the public record. In the first place, the defensive rhetoric is not entirely fraudulent. One must simply bear in mind the methods that must be used to translate conventional Orwellian mystification into plain language. The U.S. is committed to defense of the Fifth Freedom. It must therefore defend the vast domains of its influence and control from the major enemy, the indigenous population, which often has designs on what George Kennan called "our raw materials," which happen to be located in their lands. The U.S. must defend itself against "internal aggression," as another dove, Adlai Stevenson, explained in the case of Vietnam. It must "contain" Nicaragua, as agreed across the political spectrum—meaning: it must defend our little region over here from the threat of a good example. The U.S. is undoubtedly concerned to "secure" its access to the resources, both human and material, of the Grand Area, and to ensure that rivals understand that they have at best "regional responsibilities" within the "overall framework of order" maintained by the United States. There is, then, a real concern over "internal aggression" and, in recent years, the threat of rising centers of power such as Japan.

As for the superpower conflict, there is no doubt that each of the superpowers would much prefer that the other disappear, but they have long understood that this is impossible short of mutual annihilation, despite the return of rollback rhetoric among more fanatic elements today, some in the Reagan Administration. As I discussed earlier, the superpowers have settled into a system of global management called "the Cold War," in which each appeals to the threat of the global enemy to justify violence, subversion, terror and aggression in its own domains—for the U.S., much of the world. Any such act is in "defense" against the Great Satan, a standard technique of mass mobilization throughout history. Each superpower may lend support to resistance to the other's depredations (though the U.S. regards itself as having this sole prerogative, in accordance with its senior position in the partnership of global management), and there may be some quibbling about the edges. But in general the system is fairly stable in the very short-term, though fraught with immense dangers, possibly terminal catastrophe, in a longer-term framework that planners do not consider.

The defensive rhetoric is therefore in a sense quite accurate, but we have to know how to interpret and understand it. These realities reflect themselves in the military system in several ways, most obviously, in the deployment of conventional forces. About three-quarters of the Reagan military budget, for example, is devoted to conventional forces, essentially an intervention capacity required to secure the Grand Area from "internal aggression," which may be assisted by the Evil Empire at times, in accordance with the (rather fragile and immensely dangerous) rules of the Cold War.

But strategic nuclear weapons are not intended to be used in Third World intervention—though tactical nuclear weapons might be, in accordance with General Twining's precepts, and there is some evidence that the Nixon Administration contemplated the use of nuclear weapons during the Vietnam war (as Eisenhower apparently did in Korea and Vietnam) and might have proceeded to this stage had it not been for the vast growth and activism of the peace movement at the time, a point that has been developed particularly by Daniel Ellsberg. Why then is the U.S. so deeply committed to the continued improvement of strategic weapons despite the resulting threat to its own survival?

The U.S. has a deep and abiding commitment to the strategic arms race, which cannot be modified, in my opinion, short

of major institutional changes. There are two fundamental reasons. The first is that an intimidating posture is necessary to ensure that intervention can proceed with impunity under the
"nuclear umbrella"; it is for this reason that not just conventional
forces, but a strategic weapons system as well, are required for
intervention and subversion, the operative "Cold War policies."
As President Carter's Secretary of Defense Harold Brown explained to Congress in 1980, with our strategic capabilities in
place, "our other forces become meaningful instruments of military and political power." The same point was made at the same
time by Eugene Rostow, the director of the Arms Control and
Disarmament Agency in Reagan's first term. He wrote in 1979
that the U.S. nuclear arsenal is "the center of a web of relation-
ships which define the political as well as the military power of
the United States." Our nuclear forces "provide a nuclear guarantee for our interests in many parts of the world, and make it
possible for us to defend these interests by diplomacy or the use
of theater military force." They provide a "shield" for us to pursue our "global interests" by "conventional means or theater
forces"—that is, by intervention, subversion, client and mercenary states, and so on.

Much earlier, Paul Nitze, the author of NSC-68 and now influential in the Reagan Administration, had observed in a Top
Secret document (NSC-141, 1953) that Soviet advances in
weaponry might "impose greater caution in our cold war policies"
because of fear of nuclear war. Nitze therefore advocated civil
defense, which would overcome this concern, noting also that
such programs would facilitate a first strike. Civil defense being
a fantasy, it was necessary to overcome the "greater caution" by
strengthening the "nuclear shield." Notice that Nitze's same two
arguments (overcoming caution and facilitating a first strike)
carry over to the current Star Wars fantasies, but more impor-
tantly, to maintenance of a sufficiently intimidating posture so

that the "cold war policies" of intervention and subversion can be conducted without undue concern.

These considerations provide one major reason for the U.S. commitment to the arms race, but there is also a second supporting reason. The Pentagon system has long been the technique by which the state induces the public to subsidize advanced sectors of industry. The success of the state-coordinated economy during World War II taught corporate managers (who ran the wartime economy) the lesson of Keynesianism: that massive state intervention could overcome the deep crisis of capitalism. The lesson was particularly striking in the light of the failure of the much more limited New Deal measures. There are good reasons, which business elites have articulated quite clearly, why resort to the Pentagon system—in effect, a state-guaranteed market for high technology waste production combined with public subsidies for research and development—is to be preferred over other Keynesian devices, including to her methods of state support for so-called "private" enterprise. These business enterprises are "private," in that the profits are private, while the public is expected to pay the costs of research, development, protection of export markets and access to resources, a production level (generally, armaments) sufficient to provide a cushion for corporations in times of economic decline, and so on. This state-managed system of forced public subsidy is what is entitled "free enterprise" in Western ideological constructions.

Contrary to much misconception, the beneficiaries are not only, or even primarily, military industry. Thus, the basis of a modern industrial society is computers. The computer industry was subsidized by the public through the military system during the costly phase of research and development, then turned loose for profit-making when sufficient progress had been made for a market to become available. This remains true today. The substantial expenditures for the next generation of computers ("fifth generation computers") are borne by the public through the military system: the public subsidy is funneled through the Pentagon; NASA, which is largely military-related; and the Department of Energy, in charge of the production of nuclear weapons. When more advanced computers become profitable, "private" industry will market them, the public having performed its function of subsidizing the costly early stages. Much the same is true of a wide range of other advanced technologies. SDI expenditures, for example, correspond closely to those of Japan's state-coordinated industrial system, which the U.S. is unable to duplicate directly for a variety of social and historical reasons.

SDI is, in fact, almost ideal for current purposes. Like the Pentagon system more generally, it may help overcome the problem of too much consumption and a relatively low level of investment that troubles the U.S. economy: it compels the public to subsidize high technology industry. But it also helps to spur the arms race and maintain international confrontation, thus providing longer-term benefits to the system of public subsidy, private profit, through the medium of the military system.

The brilliant effectiveness of the U.S. propaganda system is revealed by its ability to appropriate the term "conservative" for the fanatic Keynesianism of the Reagan Administration, which has expanded the state sector of the economy more rapidly than at any period since World War II, mobilizing a vast public subsidy for high technology industry and incurring the predictable costs, in particular, a huge deficit, which is of little concern to the corporate planners who man the controls of the state system—though it is of growing concern to other segments of the corporate and financial elites who do not share the "après moi, le déluge" mentality of the Reaganites as they mortgage the country's future. At the same time, these "conservatives" have introduced a series of measures to strengthen the state and protect it from public scrutiny, to constrain free and open discussion, along with others that would cause mortification among conservatives, if any could be found.

The system of public subsidy to "private" industry that has developed in the postwar period has many negative consequences for the economy. It is, in the first place, highly inefficient as contrasted with the Japanese system of direct state coordination of industry geared to the commercial market. It removes intellectual and material resources from useful production to waste production for the state market with commercial viability only an incidental "spinoff." Little rational planning is possible for the longer term. Even in the narrow domain of military production, serious problems are arising, as the Pentagon is more and more compelled to rely on overseas sources (sometimes, subsidiaries of U.S.-based transnational corporations) for components of its advanced weaponry, a tendency with significant long-term implications. There is, in fact, a range of deleterious consequences, but it is not an easy matter to devise an alternative that will be consistent with the fundamental need to preserve the prerogatives of management and to ensure that the state fulfills its primary function; to serve the needs of private capital without enhancing public interests that might interfere with this central priority. And once in place, the system develops a momentum of its own as local economies and the workforce, as well as private capital, become dependent on it for survival.

Returning to the main theme, there are very good reasons why U.S. policymakers should be so committed to the race to destruction, and why questions of security or public opinion should be so marginal to national security planning. From these real world considerations one can also understand U.S. policies on arms control. The comparative advantage of the United States is no longer in production, but rather, in technological innovation—though even this is being lost, as a result of the inefficiency of the Pentagon system of public subsidy to "private" industry. The U.S. will therefore welcome reduction of nuclear armaments—a matter of minor importance, since a tiny fraction of existing arsenals would cause unacceptable destruction—as long as two basic conditions are satisfied: an intimidating posture permitting the free exercise of subversion and intervention must remain in place, and the Pentagon system of forced public subsidy to advanced sectors of industry must not be challenged. Star Wars combined with reduction of numbers of weapons is a natural U.S. stance, given the policy imperatives, though the contradictions in the weapons programs, some already discussed, may stand in the way. Appropriate strategic doctrines can be designed at will, as needed. Meanwhile, debates over the feasibility of missile defense, the choice of missiles, etc., will proceed along their largely irrelevant paths, while the race to destruction goes on.

I do not want to suggest that the real reasons for the race to destruction are entirely concealed by rhetorical flourishes about the Great Satan. As in the case of the "rotten apple theory" (the "domino theory"), the truth leaks through, now and then, as in some of the examples already cited. Corporation executives occasionally explain that we must rely on "military orders" because "defense of the home" is "one of the greatest appeals the politicians have to adjusting the system" (LTV Aerospace executive Samuel Downer). The director of Harvard University's Center for International Affairs, Professor Samuel Huntington, explains that "you may have to sell [intervention or other military actions] in such a way as to create the misimpression that it is the Soviet Union that you are fighting," as the U.S. "has done ever since the Truman Doctrine," invoked as a cover for the murderous counter-insurgency campaign in Greece in 1947. But quite generally, the educated classes succeed in concealing the true reasons, taking the official framework of discussion seriously, or at least pretending to do so.

While my focus here is on U.S. policy, it would be misleading to fail to mention that other powers, notably the USSR, make their own material contribution to the race to destruction. In the case of the Soviet Union, its military build-up, while exaggerated for propaganda purposes in the United States, is nevertheless formidable, and vastly in excess of any conceivable defensive needs. The domestic factors that drive the arms race in the USSR are not those of the United States; in particular, in a state-run command economy in a society with very limited avenues of public expression or participation, it is not necessary to resort to the military system to force a high level of investment. But there are other domestic factors that yield similar results, some of which I have briefly mentioned. The ruling military-bureaucratic elite relies ultimately on force to control the internal empire and its own citizenry, as well as the satellites—though in the latter case, it should be added, the defensive rhetoric has some substance; no government in Russia, whatever its composition, would relax controls over Eastern Europe as long as a rearmed Germany is part of a hostile Western military alliance, for historical and strategic reasons that are all too obvious.

As for Western Europe, while a neutralist option has always been a possibility, and is surely a factor impelling the popular disarmament movement there, nevertheless elite elements have an abiding commitment to the Cold War system of confrontation and militarization. Despite much fevered rhetoric, it is clear enough that they do not take the threat of Soviet attack very seriously. Western Europe has an economy far larger than that of the Soviet Union, and could deploy a military system on the scale of the USSR and the U.S. if it chose to do so. Europe also has a stake in détente because of trade and commercial patterns, quite apart from the fear of destruction. Nevertheless, occasional Soviet offers to reduce or eliminate the military blocs—how seriously intended, we do not know, since they are invariably dismissed by the West without discussion—send shivers up the spines of dominant elites in Western Europe. The basic concern is the one expressed by Jan Christiaan Smuts to Winston Churchill in 1943, which I quoted in the first lecture: "with politics let loose among those peoples, we may have a wave of disorder and wholesale Communism set going all over those parts of Europe." The pact system and the confrontation in Europe pose a serious barrier to letting politics loose among those peoples, with all sorts of possible consequences that dominant elites fear even to contemplate.

Returning to the United States, the commitment of the business-based groups that largely control the state to the race to destruction is deep and based on serious needs: to maintain a "shield" that will permit free exercise of the Cold War policies of intervention and subversion in the Grand Area, and to maintain the public subsidy to the more advanced sectors of industry. Hence the regular disregard for public opinion or even questions of survival.

It is sometimes argued that such planning is lunatic. That is true, but irrelevant. In government as in business, planning is short-range; the longer term is someone else's concern. This is natural in a competitive society, where those who do not devote themselves to short-term advantage are unlikely to be in the competition in the long run. We should not be too surprised at the fact that the U.S. made no effort to terminate the development of ICBMs—the only weapons that could seriously threaten it— or that it encourages the development of weapons such as SLCMs that will threaten it today; or that "missile gaps" and "windows of vulnerability" open and close independently of any facts; or that Reagan's SDI was advanced without any Pentagon contribution or strategic motive (that came later) and is pursued regardless of the threat to survival; or that the U.S. avoids measures such as the comprehensive test ban that would contribute to its security; and so on. These factors are not the concern of planners. Rather, their concern is to "maintain the disparity" as fully as possible, to prevent rotten apples from "infecting" others, to ensure the crucial right to rob and to exploit, to guarantee the domestic system of public subsidy, private profit, and in general, to serve the needs of the privileged and powerful sectors of domestic society.

The public may express skepticism about Star Wars and overwhelming support for a nuclear freeze and for cuts in military rather than social spending—as it does—but this too is an irrelevance, as is the clear feasibility of a comprehensive test ban and other measures that could enhance the possibilities of survival. The public has little voice in such matters, and as long as the population is quiescent, public opinion is of no more concern to elite groups that control the state apparatus than security, survival, "human rights, the raising of the living standards, and democratization." Not only the people of Latin America, but also those of the rest of the world, including the United States, are "an incident, not an end," in the phrase that so impressed Woodrow Wilson.

This is not because the leadership are "bad people," and not too much is likely to change if "better people" take their place. The reasons are institutional, and the problems must be confronted without illusions, with understanding of the social realities.

Lecture 4: Discussion March 6, 1986

QUESTION: Considering that public opinion seems irrelevant to U.S. planning and planners, and also considering the difficulty if not impossibility of bringing the type of information that you are presenting to the general public, or considering as well the probability if not the certainty of eventual world destruction, what do you suggest?

ANSWER: Tomorrow I want to talk about domestic U.S. society, what it is like inside, and that is the natural context in which to raise this question. To put it briefly, what I will suggest is the following: As long as the present institutional structures remain unchanged, the only thing (this is for people of the U.S., it is not addressed to Nicaraguans) we can do is to try to slow down the worst catastrophes. That means to try to block the next crazy weapons system and try to block the next intervention in the Third World, knowing that all we are doing is putting a band-aid on a cancer. You just do that because you want the world to exist a little longer and because you have the responsibility to try to protect people who are being tortured and murdered. That is what is called a "holding action." What has to be done ultimately is to change the institutions. That is a big task.

QUESTION: Professor Chomsky, I would like you to comment on the U.S. national budget in 1984-1985. How much was given to the military, education, welfare, and health? These four things, and because we in Nicaragua—there is a tremendous amount of the national budget for the military for defense. To see how we compare in two different situations. The U.S. does not have an army of "contras" attacking them as we have in Nicaragua.

ANSWER: I can't give you the exact numbers for two reasons. For one, I don't really remember them, and for another, they're very hard to discover. So, the military budget is not just the Pentagon budget. There's an agency of the U.S. government called the Department of Energy—that sounds nice and constructive, everyone wants energy. In fact, it is the agency that makes nuclear weapons. And there's an agency called NASA, theoretically concerned with exploration of space for scientific purposes. It's basically part of the Pentagon. And there are all sorts of other things which are part of the military system. It is very hard to make a precise calculation, but you can make some calculations and it's possible that the actual military budget runs to something in the neighborhood of 10% of the GNP. Now that's much less than Nicaragua but the U.S. is a fantastically rich country, so these numbers don't mean very much.

About your other point—again, I don't have the actual figures, but the general picture is that under Reagan the entire state system has gone up. Most of that increase is in the military system. Meanwhile, the welfare system has deteriorated very rapidly, and in fact other things have deteriorated too—support for civil rights, for example. There are laws which require the State Executive to support certain programs. For example, it must protect the right of people to vote in, say, Alabama. Well, the Government just stopped doing these things, and what has happened is that private civil rights organizations have had to take over the role of the State in enforcing the law.

There's a very respectable and conservative organization in the U.S. called the American Civil Liberties Union (the ACLU). They have had to take on the task of enforcing the law on such matters as voting rights or women's rights, and the whole legal system which the government is just refusing to enforce. So private charitable organizations like the ACLU have had to do it through the courts, which is very inefficient.

In fact, I'll finish with a little story: one of the things the Reagan Administration is trying to do is to sell off part of the national economy. For example, there is in the U.S. a barely functioning railroad system, partially subsidized, partially owned by the government. They want to sell it to promote private enterprise, so then it can be used to make a profit by sending freight instead of people, which is very inefficient. If you want to send freight, you can fill up a whole car, but people object to being sent like that. That is happening with lots of things. It's a way of cutting down public services. Last December, the ACLU issued a public statement in which they offered to buy the Justice Department. They said the Reagan Administration isn't enforcing the law, so why don't you let us buy it, since we're the ones trying to enforce the law anyway. Well, as I've mentioned many times, the U.S. is a very disciplined society so this never made the press, as far as I know.

LECTURE 5

The Domestic Scene

I would like to conclude these lectures with some comments about U.S. society itself, asking how state policies are fashioned and what possibilities there are of modifying them. The basic question reduces to this: To what extent is the United States a democratic society, in which the general population is able to influence public policy? There is no simple answer to this question. It is one that has many dimensions. Let us consider a few of these.

One crucial dimension in terms of which one can evaluate the democratic credentials of some political system has to do with the power of the state to coerce its citizens and protect itself from their scrutiny and control, its power to prevent free expression and free association, to maintain state secrets and conduct its affairs without public awareness and influence. Such questions were vigorously debated in the early years of the Republic after the U.S. War of Independence. If the people are sovereign, libertarians argued, then the state must be subordinated to them, not conversely. If, for example, legislators have the constitutional right of free expression with immunity from prosecution, then citizens should have no less a right: specifically, they should be free to condemn the government and its practices without fear of prosecution for "seditious libel," the doctrine that the state can be criminally assaulted by mere speech and writing, short of action, and that the state has the right to punish this crime through the courts or the Parliament. It is a remarkable fact, worth remembering, that through the 18th century there was virtually no challenge to this doctrine of the common law, which was accepted as legitimate by leading advocates of libertarian ideals: John Milton, John Locke, Benjamin Franklin, Thomas Jefferson, and others. Few even went so far as to declare truth to be a defense against libel; in fact true charges were regarded as even more culpable, since they brought authority into disrepute and threatened civil order. The struggle is far from over, even in the Western industrial democracies, where it is most advanced. This is, of course, only one of the many aspects of the question of the locus of sovereignty in the political system and the rights accorded to the people and to the state authorities.

Along this dimension, the United States is near the libertarian extreme in the spectrum of existing societies. Relatively speaking, the United Stares is a free and open society, in which the state has limited means of coercion to exercise against its own citizens. This is a very important fact. It means that an aroused public can influence policy in many ways, ranging from political action to civil disobedience and resistance. It is also possible to learn a good deal about the government, its plans and its practices. In these respects, the U.S. is probably more free and open than any other society in the world. Despite flaws in practice, the protection granted to citizens by the Bill of Rights, and in more recent years, the rights afforded by the Freedom of Information Act (which permits wide access to state documents), are unusual if not unique among existing political systems. It is not surprising that statist reactionaries of the Reaganite variety are seeking to abridge these rights as part of their project of aggrandizement of the state and expansion of its power.

In these respects, the United States is at the opposite extreme in the world spectrum from the second superpower, a closed society in which the state is protected from scrutiny and has ample means to coerce the population.

Along this crucial dimension, then, the United States is among the most free societies in the world, and it will remain so despite Reaganite assaults on individual freedom and efforts to enhance state power. This is, again, a critical and important fact. We may note, however, that there is little reason to expect a correlation between the internal freedom of some society and its external violence and repression, and history reveals no such correlation. A society that is relatively free and open at home may be brutal and murderous abroad.

Why may we be fairly confident that despite the efforts of reactionary elements of the Reaganite variety, the state will remain limited in its power to coerce and control? The answer can be found in broader aspects of U.S. society. The United States is a capitalist democracy, to the extent that such a concept is meaningful (the extent is limited, since capitalism poses severe barriers to meaningful democracy, a matter to which I will turn in a moment). Of course, the U.S. is not truly a capitalist society; no such system could long survive, for reasons that have been well understood, most clearly within business circles, for a century. Business demands that the state intervene in the economy to regulate markets and otherwise support business interests, and also that it employ its means of violence in the international arena in the manner described by Woodrow Wilson in the private papers I cited in the first lecture, among other services the state must provide for the wealthy and privileged. On the other hand, business does not want the state to be a powerful competitor, interfering with the prerogatives of the businessman or organizing popular forces that might act in the parliamentary arena or elsewhere to counter business dominance of the society. Thus, business has long had a love-hate relation to the state: it wants a strong state to serve its needs, a state capable of intervening in domestic affairs and the international system; it wants a weak state that will not interfere with private privilege, but will enhance it. To a large extent, political debate in a capitalist democracy such as the United States reduces to efforts on the part of various segments of the business community to resolve this problem in a way that will suit their sometimes conflicting interests within a shared consensus.

Though remote from the ideal, the U.S. is closer in many respects to a capitalist order than other leading industrial democracies. In a capitalist system, everything tends to become a commodity, including freedom: you can have as much of it as you can buy. The wealthy and privileged therefore have an interest in maintaining personal freedom and limiting the coercive power of the state, since they are the prime beneficiaries. For Black teen-agers in the ghetto, the system of formal liberties has little significance, since they have only limited access to it—and again, reactionaries of the Reaganite variety attempt to limit this access still further by undermining legal aid to the poor, reducing legal constraints on police power, and so on. The wealthy and privileged will defend personal freedom from state encroachment, though in times of rising class struggle and domestic challenge to their effective rule, this may change. Given the interest of dominant elites in limiting state power, we can be fairly confident that individual rights will withstand the onslaughts of statist reactionaries. One consequence is that dissident minorities also benefit from the freedom defended by the privileged, roughly to the extent that they share in existing privilege. And in a wealthy society like the United States, that includes a substantial part of the population, in greater or lesser degree.

A second crucial dimension along which democratic credentials can be evaluated is simply this: Who makes the basic decisions about what happens within the society and how it acts in the international arena? Here we may distinguish two major categories of decisions: investment decisions and political decisions. The former have to do with what is produced, how it is produced, what work is done, how production and profits are distributed and to whom, how the conditions of work are managed and controlled, and so on. The second category has to do with state policy: which groups actually participate in shaping it?

As far as investment decisions are concerned, in law and in practice they are excluded from popular control in the United States, which does not aspire to democracy in the full sense but only to *capitalist* democracy, something rather different. To 18th century libertarians, the prime enemies of freedom were the feudal system, slavery and two powerful institutions: the Church and the State. They could envision a social order in which individuals (more accurately, white male property owners) would be more or less equal and free, once these barriers to liberty were removed. They could not foresee the centralization of effective power in the industrial and financial system of corporate capitalism. To apply their libertarian ideals to the modern world, one must go far beyond a concern for the coercive role of the Church and the State. The true inheritors of classical liberalism, in my view, are the libertarian socialists and anarchists, who oppose hierarchic structures and authoritarian institutions in a far broader realm.

In a capitalist democracy, the primary concern of everyone must be to ensure that the wealthy are satisfied; all else is secondary. Unless the wants of investors are satisfied, there is no production, no work, no resources available for welfare, in short, no possibility of survival. It is not a matter of "all or none," but "more or less." Only to the extent that the demands of the wealthy—those who control investment decisions—are satisfied can the population at large hope for a decent existence in their role as servants of private power, who rent themselves to those who own and manage the private economy. This too is a factor of fundamental importance.

Another feature of a capitalist democracy such as the United States is the inequity in distribution of resources, which translates into vast differences in the ability to participate in a meaningful way even in the narrow margin of decisions that remain within the political system. Furthermore, the political system, like every other aspect of capitalist democracy, must be dedicated to ensuring that the demands of the wealthy are satisfied, or the society will decline and collapse. The threat to withhold investment, or capital flight, can suffice to set very narrow limits for decisions within the political system, a fact of which Latin Americans are well aware.

In the real world, state policy is largely determined by those groups that command resources, ultimately by virtue of their ownership and management of the private economy or their status as wealthy professionals. The major decision-making positions in the Executive branch of the government are typically filled by representatives of major corporations, banks and investment firms, a few law firms that cater primarily to corporate interests and thus represent the broad interests of owners and managers rather than some parochial interest, and selected intellectuals who become "experts," as Henry Kissinger once explained without irony, by virtue of their ability to articulate the consensus of the powerful and to manage their affairs for them. The Legislative branch is more varied, but overwhelmingly, it is drawn from the business and professional classes. This has, in fact, been true since the 1780s, when for a brief period, before the Republic was fully formed, legislators were drawn from a wide range of social strata. If a Senator or Representative leaves Congress, he (or occasionally, she) will not return to a position as industrial worker, small farmer, truck driver, clerk, etc., but, typically, to a business or law firm. Accordingly, in their commitments, associations and perceptions of social reality, legislators represent the business and wealthy professional classes.

Furthermore, the external conditions of policy formation are set by the same narrow elite of privileged groups. They carry out the planning studies, finance the political parties, dominate Washington lobbying, and in a variety of other ways, determine the conditions within which the political system functions.

In short, a capitalist democracy is, at best, a very limited form of democracy.

All of this has long been understood. John Jay, the President of the Continental Congress and the first Chief Justice of the U.S. Supreme Court, held that "the people who own the country ought to govern it." The political system as well as the social system was designed to serve the needs of the propertied classes; others might benefit incidentally, as conditions allowed. And so affairs have proceeded since. The United States, while unusual among industrial democracies in the relative inability of the state to coerce its citizens and protect itself from their scrutiny, is also unusual in the narrowness of choice afforded within the political system. There is no political party based on labor and the poor, responsive to some extent to their needs and interests and committed to limited reforms of the capitalist system, such as the socialist, labor, or Communist parties in Europe. To a large degree, the U.S. is a one-party state, where the ruling party has two factions that compete for control of the government. U.S. political history is, to a significant extent, a history of conflict among those in a position to make investment decisions; where few major issues divide them, there is a period of political harmony, and where such issues do arise, there is political conflict over them. The general public is afforded an opportunity to ratify elite decisions, but the option of participating in making them is limited, very largely, to privileged elites.

Much of the public is aware of its marginalization and of the essential irrelevance of the political system to its concerns. Close to half the electorate does not even take the trouble to go to the polls in Presidential elections, and of those who vote, many do so independently of the public stand of the candidates on crucial

issues. Take the most recent (1984) Presidential election, for example. This is almost invariably described as a landslide victory
for Ronald Reagan and his "conservatism"—actually, a form of
reactionary jingoism that would be anathema to true conservatives. In fact, there was no such "land slide." Reagan received less
than 30% of the potential vote. Of those who voted for Reagan,
about 60% felt that his legislative program would harm the country, while about I % of the electorate voted for him because they
considered him a "real conservative."

Polls taken after the election showed that half the public believe that the government is run "by a few big interests looking
out for themselves." As always, voting was highly skewed towards
privileged sectors, much higher among white collar than blue collar workers, and very low among the poor and unemployed, who
evidently do not consider themselves to be represented within
the political system. These facts are particularly noteworthy in
the light of the extraordinary efforts "to bring out the vote" and
the unremitting patriotic propaganda about the magnificence of
American democracy. The rather accurate conceptions of half
the population would be castigated as "extremist" or "Marxist"
if they were to receive articulate expression. But much of the
population understands the accuracy of John Jay's dictum, despite the dedicated efforts undertaken within the doctrinal system to convince them otherwise.

Although I know of no direct study of the question, it is a
fair guess that as level of education increases, the level of understanding of these social realities will decline. We see evidence for
this conclusion in that these topics can barely be discussed within
the ideological institutions managed by the educated classes: the
media, the schools, the universities, the journals of opinion. In a
rare moment of candor, the Trilateral Commission study on the
"Crisis of Democracy," which I mentioned earlier, described the
schools and universities as among the institutions responsible for

"the indoctrination of the young." Those who are more subject to indoctrination, which continues in later life through the media, journals, popular and often scholarly books, are more likely to be subject to its illusions. Furthermore, the educated classes are not only the main targets of the system of indoctrination but also its practitioners; their self-interest dictates that they adopt and believe its doctrines, if they are to be able to fulfill their role as educators, journalists, or "responsible intellectuals" with access to privilege, influence, and respect. What is more, the victims of the system of exploitation develop an intuitive understanding of reality through their own lives. The banality, superficiality and often sheer silliness of cultivated discourse therefore comes as little surprise.

For those who care to consider the factual record, there is no dearth of evidence to support the cynicism about the political system that is evidently widespread among the less educated segments of the population. In 1964, for example, one primary issue in the electoral campaign was escalation of the war in Vietnam. This was overwhelmingly opposed by the electorate, who voted by a margin of 2 to 1 for the candidate who declared that he would not escalate the war—while he was then engaged in plans to do exactly that, as we now know, and as he proceeded to do immediately upon election. Similarly, when Ronald Reagan took office in 1980, Congress and the President, allegedly responding to a "conservative" mandate, set to work to dismantle the welfare state measures (limited, by European standards) that had been instituted since the New Deal and under the pressure of the growing popular movements of the 1960s. Meanwhile in poll after poll, the population registered its opposition to these steps by very large margins. Polls consistently reveal that the public favors cutbacks in military rather than social programs, and even favors increased taxes if these are necessary for the programs of social welfare, environmental protection, work safety standards,

women's rights, urban aid, etc., that the public overwhelmingly
endorsed as they were disappearing from view. In a recent survey
of public opinion polls, Thomas Ferguson and Joel Rogers conclude that "on virtually all the important issues identified with
the 'Reagan revolution' in public policy, public opinion ran
against the President." Exactly as in the case of security policy,
which I discussed yesterday, public opinion is a mere irrelevance
as long as the population is quiescent and subdued. Congress
and the President were responding to other voices, not a public
mandate as conventional doctrine holds.

There have been attempts to overcome the marginalization
of the general population within the political system. Thus in the
late 19th century, the Populist movement began to develop as
an independent political force, representing elements beyond
privileged elites. It elicited a sharp reaction from the dominant
business circles, and was quickly eliminated from the scene. Its
demise led to a large migration to Canada from the states with
agrarian radical movements, a significant contribution to the
Canadian social democratic movement, which has no real counterpart in the United Stares. Labor organizing has also been a
hard and bitter struggle. Its history in the United States is one
of considerable violence by the state and private power. We may
recall that May Day was initially an international demonstration
of solidarity with U.S. labor struggles. Social realities in the U.S.
are illustrated by the fact that in the U.S. all memory of this has
disappeared, and May Day is now not a labor holiday but the
occasion for jingoist pronouncements. It is "Law Day," the day
on which Reagan announces that the U.S. will refuse to accept
the judgment of the World Court and declares a "national emergency" and an embargo against Nicaragua.

Furthermore, the huge public relations industry in the United
States has devoted its quite impressive efforts, since its origins
early in the century, to undermining the labor movement and to

protecting investment decisions and corporate power from public control. The result is what the Australian scholar Alex Carey describes as "a propaganda-managed democracy" in which the so-called "free enterprise system" is identified "in popular consciousness with every cherished value," while "interventionist welfare-oriented governments and strong unions (the only agencies capable of checking the complete domination of society by the corporations)" are identified with "tyranny, oppression and even subversion." Meanwhile, of course, the enormous and increasing role of the state in subsidizing "free enterprise" and serving its needs is suppressed. "Anti-Communism" has been used as a highly effective device to control the labor movement, with the cooperation of labor leaders, who have presided over the decline of unions in the United States to well under 20% of the labor force while working energetically to undermine labor unity and independence from state capitalist control abroad as well, including Central America. The "Red Scare" after World War I and the post-World War II attack on labor and civil rights (often mislabelled "McCarthyism") involved state repression as well as a massive propaganda assault coordinated by business groups, which have an unusually high degree of class consciousness in the United States, and work effectively to ensure that they are alone in this regard. The intelligentsia also lent their talents enthusiastically to the cause after World War II, abandoning the earlier illusion that they might gain a measure of power by riding a wave of popular struggle (the Leninist dream) and recognizing that real power, and the basis for their privilege, would continue to reside in the business sectors that dominate the state capitalist system.

The 1960s and early 1970s again witnessed the growth of popular activism and popular movements that might have threatened business control of the political system, with the rise of the civil rights movement, the anti-war movement, the feminist movement, ethnic movements, organization of local communities, and so on. These developments evoked immediate and serious concern on the part of elite groups. They constituted the "crisis" identified by the liberal Trilateral Commission as a major threat to "democracy," as the term is understood within the reigning doctrinal system. As one participant in the Trilateral Commission study remarked, "Truman had been able to govern the country with the cooperation of a relatively small number of Wall Street lawyers and bankers," but these happy days—when there was no "crisis of democracy"—seemed to be passing as popular-based groups began to enter the political arena.

To counter this "crisis of democracy," a several-pronged offensive was launched by privileged elites. It included an enormous growth of business lobbying; a reversal of the temporary and very limited opening of the media that reflected the growth of the popular movements; a proliferation of "think tanks" and a general propaganda campaign to restrict the political agenda to the needs of the powerful; an assault against labor and civil rights on the part of the Reagan Administration (which largely represents these elite anti-democratic forces); major steps to undermine welfare state measures and to expand the military system; and an "activist" foreign policy of renewed intervention, subversion, and outright international terrorism abroad. The goal was to overcome the effects of "the crisis of democracy" and to restore the public to its proper condition of apathy and obedience while the political system remains a game played among privileged elites.

The main themes of the propaganda system in the post-Vietnam period reflect this agenda. By the early 1970s, a large majority of the population had come to understand that the U.S. government was engaged in major crimes. Some way had to be found to restore the mythology of "American benevolence" that had served for so many years to mobilize the population in support of state violence. Since the criminal acts of the state could not be denied, it was necessary to show that they were merely defects of a flawed personal leadership that deviated from the path of righteousness, not a reflection of U.S. institutions acting in accord with longstanding historical patterns. Nixon's petty criminality was brilliantly exploited to achieve this end. In fact, Nixon's real crimes were carefully excluded from the Watergate affair. There was much outrage over Nixon's "enemies list," which included powerful figures in elite circles along with others whose presence would have aroused no interest; but the fact that under the Nixon Administration the national political police (the FBI) had taken part in the assassination of the Black Panther organizer Fred Hampton in Chicago was not raised in the Watergate proceedings. It is a crime to call powerful people bad names in private (nothing happened to anyone on the "enemies list"; I know, having been on it myself), but not to assassinate a Black organizer. A bungled raid on the Democratic Party headquarters by a Nixon-related group was the centerpiece of the Watergate charges. At the very same time, secret documents were released showing that the FBI had been engaged in similar practices against the Socialist Workers Party (a legal political party) since the Kennedy Administration, alongside of criminal actions undertaken to undermine popular movements, to foment violence in the ghettoes, and so on. But these matters, far more serious than the charges against Nixon, were put aside, since to pursue them would have led beyond the merely personal defects of one bad man to institutional critique, which is quite intolerable. The "secret bombing" of Cambodia did not appear in the bill of indictment. It was mentioned in the proceedings; the "crime," however, was not the murderous attack on a peasant society with tens of thousands killed, but rather the fact that Congress had not been properly informed. For his crimes, Nixon was expelled from the body politic, now purified and prepared to return to its traditional vocation of "international goodwill."

The congressional human rights program, which reflected the significant improvement in the moral and intellectual climate brought about by the popular movements of the 1960s, was also seized upon by the propaganda system, which declared under Carter that human rights are "the Soul of our foreign policy." This grand commitment did not prevent the Carter Administration from supporting with enthusiasm the massacre of tens of thousands of Timorese in a U.S.-backed invasion, the murderous bombing of southern Lebanon by a U.S. client, the Somoza and Marcos regimes, and on, and on; meanwhile Carter was accused of undermining "our friends" while excusing "our enemies." By the time Reagan took office, it was assumed that the dread "Vietnam syndrome" had been overcome, and "the Soul of our foreign policy" shifted to the struggle against "international terrorism," narrowly defined to exclude the central U.S. role in engendering this "plague of the modern era," and with ample falsification and deceit to "prove" that the plague was part of the Kremlin-inspired conspiracy to take all we have.

The record shows considerable enterprise and ingenuity on the part of the propaganda system. And it had its effects, undeniably, though less so among the population at large than is generally believed.

One may detect an analogy between the fears aroused by the "crisis of democracy" at home and in such dependencies as El Salvador, where the growth of popular organizations in the 1970s also elicited grave concern, as we have seen. The response of elite groups to the "crisis of democracy" at home and abroad naturally differs. In El Salvador, the crisis was overcome by calling out the death squads. At home, more subtle means are required.

The basic point is one that I have already mentioned. Meaningful democracy must be based on an organizational structure that permits isolated individuals to enter the domain of decision-making by pooling their limited resources, educating themselves and others, and formulating ideas and programs that they can place on the political agenda and work to realize. In the absence of such organizations, political democracy is the domain of elite groups that command resources, based ultimately on their control of the private economy. At best, the range of possibilities is limited in a capitalist democracy in which the public is excluded from participation in the basic decisions concerning production and work. But even limited steps towards effective political democracy are perceived as extremely threatening within the narrow circles of the privileged and powerful, and in the post-Vietnam era they have once again devoted very considerable energies to avert this threat to elite dominance.

I have mentioned two central dimensions along which the democratic credentials of some sociopolitical system may be evaluated: the power of the state to coerce its citizens and to protect itself from their control; the locus of decision-making in the social, economic and political systems. A third crucial dimension has to do with the ideological system. To what extent are ordinary people able to become informed, a prerequisite to democratic participation? I have addressed this question repeatedly throughout these lectures. The right of free expression is vigorously maintained in the United States, in that state controls are very weak by comparative standards. On the other hand, the ideological system operates within very narrow constraints and those who do not accept them are effectively excluded. Debate is permitted, even encouraged, as long as it adopts the fundamental principles of the ideological system. In the case of the Vietnam war, for example, when it was clear that the costs to the U.S. were mounting severely, it became possible to debate the issue of the war in the national press, but only within certain limits. One could take the position of the hawks, who held that with sufficient dedication the U.S. could win, or the position of the doves, who held that success was unlikely though "we all pray" that the hawks are right and we will "all be saluting the wisdom and statesmanship of the American government" in conducting a war that was turning Vietnam into "a land of ruin and wreck" if the hawks prove to be right in their judgment, as explained by historian Arthur Schlesinger, regarded as an "antiwar leader" in the establishment media. Those who held that aggression was wrong even if it could succeed were systematically excluded from the discussion. To this day, as I have already mentioned, there is no such event as the U.S. attack against South Vietnam in official history, though this was clearly the central element in the Indochina war.

Much the same is true in other cases, some already discussed. The debate—such as it is—over Nicaragua today in the mainstream is a revealing example. As I pointed out in the third lecture in reviewing the national press, debate is tolerated, but within very narrow limits. Recall that in the crucial first three months of 1986, as debate was heating up over the impending vote on contra aid in Congress, the two major national newspapers assured 100 percent uniformity on the central issue, permitting nothing sympathetic to the Sandinista government. There was no mention at all of the not-insignificant fact that in sharp contrast to U.S. clients in the region, the Sandinistas do not slaughter their own population; Sandinista social reforms, the prime reason for the U.S. attack, merited two passing phrases. Editorial commentary since 1980 is similar, as I noted. While the imposition of a State of Siege in Nicaragua in October 1985 elicited outraged denunciations, the *renewal* of the Salvadoran State of Siege two days later passed without comment; indeed, it has never been mentioned in a *New York Times* editorial. All of this is particularly instructive in the light of the unquestionable fact that the Salvadoran State of Siege has been applied with incomparably greater harshness since it was instituted in 1980, and that unlike Nicaragua, El Salvador is not under attack by the regional superpower.

Elsewhere, I have examined press coverage on these and other issues in greater derail, as have others. The results are quite regularly the same: suppression or apologetics with regard to crimes of the United Stares and its clients; anguish and outrage, often based on the kind of flimsy evidence that would be dismissed with contempt if adduced in connection with the U.S. and its diems, or on outright fabrication, with regard to the crimes of official enemies. One expects to find such behavior in the official press of a totalitarian state. The extent to which much the same is true in a press that operates without overt state controls will come as a surprise and a shock to those who choose to inquire into the matter honestly. Documentation of this matter is quite extensive, but invariably ignored as much too inconvenient in discussion of the nature of the media, which are—the ultimate irony—regularly condemned for their "adversarial " stance with regard to state and private power.

The reasons for the systematic deference of the media towards external power are not difficult to discern. The media represent the same interests that control the state and private economy, and it is therefore not very surprising to discover that they generally act to confine public discussion and understanding to the needs of the powerful and privileged. The media are, in the first place, major corporations. Their primary market is business (advertisers), and like other corporations, they must bend to the needs of the community of investors. In the unlikely event that they might seek to pursue an independent path, they would quickly be called to account, and could not survive. Their top management (editors, etc.) is drawn from the ranks of wealthy professionals who tend naturally to share the perceptions of the privileged and powerful, and who have achieved their position, and maintain it, by having demonstrated their efficiency in the task of serving the needs of dominant elites. Furthermore, by virtue of their associations, class status, aspirations, and so on, they tend to share the perceptions and commitments of those who hold effective power. Thus it is only to be expected that the framework of interpretation, selection of what counts as "news," permitted opinion, etc., will fall well within the range that conforms to the needs of the nexus of state-private power that controls the economy and the political system.

Journalists and columnists have the choice of conforming or being excluded, and in a wealthy society, the rewards for conformity can be substantial. Those who choose to conform, hence to remain within the system, will soon find that they internalize the beliefs and attitudes that they express and that shape their work; it is a very rare individual who can believe one thing and say another on a regular basis. A certain range of opinion is tolerated, generally on narrow tactical questions within a shared consensus as to "the national interest," and one should not discount the professional integrity of the better and more honest journalists. But the institutional structure of the system is in its essence hostile to independence of mind, and it is hardly surprising that it is so rarely exhibited. The point is not that the journalists or commentators are dishonest; rather, unless they happen to conform to the institutional requirements, they will find no place in the corporate media. At the margins of the system—e.g., in the listener-supported local radio—one can find deviation from the prevailing norms, and there are deviations amounting to "statistical error" even within the mainstream on occasion, but these norms, rooted in the institutional structure, are very rarely violated. With some variations, much the same is true in the schools and universities, for similar reasons.

As in the case of the political system, the United States is unusual among the capitalist democracies in the ideological constraints observed by the media. One would be hard put to find even a mild democratic socialist in the mass media, and a genuine opposition press is difficult to imagine. In these respects, the

United States departs from the norm among capitalist democracies, for a variety of reasons that I cannot pursue here—one of them being its power and importance in the global system. Hence the two major principles that I mentioned in the first lecture and have sought to illustrate throughout—the commitment of the state to serving private power in the domestic and international arena, and the commitment of the ideological institutions to limiting popular understanding of social reality— are firmly rooted in the institutional structure of the society and are highly resistant to change. The conformism of articulate U.S. opinion has long been recognized by observers with their eyes open. Sixty years after the American revolution, Alexis de Tocqueville commented on the "universal conformity" he found in the United States, observing that "I know of no country in which there is so little true independence of mind and freedom of discussion as in America." Citing these remarks in a review of the post-revolutionary era, historian Lawrence Friedman comments that "there was no vigorous, effective, or even noticeable tradition of dissent against spread-eagle patriotism in the New Nation." The cult of personality constructed about George Washington and the Founding Fathers in general reached particularly ludicrous extremes, and still does. In 1858, Henry David Thoreau, one of the rare dissidents, wrote in his journal that:

> There is no need of a law to check the license of the press. It is law enough, and more than enough, to itself. Virtually, the community have come together and agreed what things shall be uttered, have agreed on a platform and to excommunicate him who departs from it, and not one in a thousand dares utter anything else.

It would be more accurate to say that not one in a thousand is able to think any thing else, so effectively has the system of thought control worked its magic.

In the 20th century, the commitment to thought control became quite self-conscious. It was recognized by leading political scientists, journalists, representatives of the rising Public Relations industry, and others, that in a country where the voice of the people can be heard, it is necessary to ensure that that voice says the right things. In a state based on internal violence, it suffices to control what people do; what they think is a matter of little significance, as long as they can be controlled, ultimately by force. Where state violence is more limited, it becomes necessary to control what people think as well. There is, in short, a connection between the freedom from state coercion in the United States and the remarkable effectiveness of the system of thought control. And this fact has often been explicitly recognized in elite circles, who have emphasized the importance of "manufacture of consent" (the distinguished journalist and political commentator Walter Lippmann) or "engineering of consent" (Edward Bernays, the highly respected leading figure in the Public Relations industry) to ensure that the population will ratify the decisions of far-sighted leaders, who must be free from influence by the unwashed masses.

One of the rare critics of these conceptions, political scientist Robert Dahl, wrote that "if one assumes that political preferences are simply plugged into the system by leaders (business or other) in order to extract what they want from the system, then the model of plebiscitary democracy is substantially equivalent to the model of totalitarian rule." Generally, however, the necessity for thought control is accepted by those who consider the matter; most merely adopt it passively as the norm. It is not surprising, then, that the liberal Trilateral Commission should warn about the danger of critical analysis of the institutions responsible "for the indoctrination of the young"—the schools and universities, in particular.

The devices of "manufacture of consent" are more subtle than the propaganda measures adopted within totalitarian societies, where rule is maintained by the bludgeon. They are also probably more effective. One of the most effective devices is to encourage debate, but within a system of unspoken presuppositions that incorporate the basic principles of the doctrinal system. These principles are therefore removed from inspection; they become the framework for thinkable thought, not objects of rational consideration. The more the debate rages within permissible bounds, the more effectively the unquestioned premises are instilled as sacred Truths. I have given many examples in the course of this discussion, and many more in print, probably thousands of pages by now, as have others. None of this can possibly be understood—indeed, the words cannot even be heard—within respectable intellectual circles in the United States.

We should not be surprised, then, that despite the openness of the society, the basic elements of policy planning and their historical patterns are obscured and concealed by the media and much of scholarship, and that the rich documentary record of planning should be known only in narrow circles, and there rarely understood. Nor should we be surprised that representatives of the major U.S. media are incapable of discovering the contra atrocities quickly unearthed by journalists from other countries or by human rights investigators, or that social reforms in Nicaragua should be effaced from the historical record along with the 1984 elections (which did not take place), that the U.S. attack on South Vietnam never occurred, and so on, endlessly. Journalists and other commentators either consciously understand the path to success, or so successfully internalize the doctrines of the faith that they become unable to think unacceptable thoughts. Rare exceptions exist, and can even be tolerated at the margins, where rational discussion appears to be some form of incomprehensible madness, so remote is it from what is drilled into everyone's head day after day by the propaganda system.

The system of manufacture of consent is highly successful, at least among the educated classes. The effects on the general population are less clear, but the matter is unimportant as long as they remain passive and quiescent and do not create any "crisis of democracy." There is evidence that a considerable gulf exists between popular opinion and the doctrines espoused by the well-disciplined educated classes. I have mentioned a few examples. To take another, consider attitudes towards the war in Vietnam. It is widely believed that criticism of the war was spear headed by the media and the educated classes in general. This is entirely false. Opposition to the war developed in a climate of extreme hostility on the part of articulate liberal intellectuals and the media. It was not until business circles began to turn against the war because of its costs that articulate critique became a noticeable phenomenon, and even then it was bounded in the manner I have already mentioned within the mainstream and respectable circles in general. The illusion developed because the voices of criticism that were finally heard, as a result of the mass popular activism, were generally those of the tiny minority of educated and privileged people associated with the popular movements, quite naturally. But they were not "its leaders" and they were far from representative of the intellectual community, contrary to many current fantasies.

An indication of the real facts was given by an in-depth study of attitudes of "the American intellectual elite" undertaken in the spring of 1970, at the height of opposition to the war after the U.S. invasion of Cambodia, with universities shut down after student protests and popular dissidence reaching proportions that were quite frightening to elite groups. The results showed that virtually all were opposed to the war and would have been classified as doves. But when we turn to the reasons, we find that the overwhelming majority were opposed on "pragmatic grounds"— the war would not succeed in its aims—while a minority were opposed because the war was becoming too bloody (what the study called "moral grounds"): a certain amount of killing, maiming and torture is legitimate, but too much may offend delicate souls. Principled opposition to the war was so negligible as to be barely detectable. Perhaps 1 percent of the sample opposed the war on the grounds that aggression is wrong, even if undertaken by the United States. On the other hand, if the same sample of intellectuals had been asked their opinions about the Soviet invasion of Czechoslovakia, all would have opposed it on these principled grounds (obviously it could not be opposed on "pragmatic grounds," since it worked, or on "moral grounds," since casualties were slight). But in the case of the United States, principle must be abandoned entirely, or one loses one's status as a respectable intellectual. A survey of the German General Staff after Stalingrad might have yielded similar results. Notice again that the abandonment of principle was not a matter of conscious deceit; rather, among elite intellectuals, the idea that the U.S. is engaged in aggression in its attack on South Vietnam, or that such an exercise might be wrong in principle, or even that such an event took place, is simply unthinkable; the words cannot be heard, even today.

In contrast, much of the general population opposed the war on grounds of principle. As late as the 1980s, after a decade of dedicated efforts to overcome the "Vietnam syndrome," over 70% of the population regard the war as "fundamentally wrong and immoral," not merely "a mistake" as the official doves maintain, a position held by far fewer "opinion leaders" (a group that includes clergy, etc.), and by a tiny minority of intellectuals even at the height of anti-war protest. Similar results hold in many other cases, for example, the 1982 Israeli invasion of Lebanon, approved by a margin of about 3 to 2 by more educated people, opposed by about the same margin by less educated people, who are capable of understanding that aggression and massacre are aggression and massacre, not a legitimate act of self-defense in accord with the highest ideals of Western civilization.

What actually happened during the Vietnam war protest is instructive. A mass popular movement developed, spontaneously, without organization or centralized leadership, taking many forms, and in an atmosphere of extreme hostility on the part of the media and articulate opinion in general. As I described in the second lecture, it reached such a scale that the government was unable to undertake a true national mobilization, as during World War II, but was compelled to fight a "guns-and-butter" war. But the scale of the attack was such that this led to serious consequences for the U.S. economy, which began to decline relative to its real rivals: Europe and Japan. Furthermore, the U.S. army, much to its credit, began to collapse from within, reflecting the dissidence within the domestic society. The Tet offensive in January 1968 convinced major business circles that the investment should be liquidated; it was simply not worth the costs, including the emerging "crisis of democracy" and the deleterious economic effects. A delegation of "wise men" was dispatched to Washington to call for a gradual reduction of the U.S. involvement, a shift to a more capital-intensive war with most of the U.S. troops withdrawn and steps towards a negotiated settlement. About a year later, criticism of the war became legitimate in the media, though within the bounds already discussed. The consequences I have also discussed.

Much the same was true in connection with Central America. The Reagan Administration took office with the clear intent of moving towards direct military intervention in El Salvador. The February 1981 White Paper, with its fanciful claims about aggression by Nicaragua as an agency of the Kremlin-directed conspiracy, was a clear announcement of these plans. It was assumed that the "Vietnam syndrome" had been overcome so that the U.S. could return to its historical pattern of direct intervention, a conclusion that was not unreasonable in the light of articulate opinion. The White Paper was greeted with skepticism or derision in

Europe, but accepted in the U.S. media as Higher Truth. There was, however, an unanticipated negative popular reaction at an impressive scale, with demonstrations and protests, spontaneous and unorganized, with the Churches now playing a serious role. The Administration backed away from its fiery rhetoric, fearing that more central programs, such as the program of militarization of U.S. society, might be threatened. Some time later, the media began to criticize the White Paper, and for a brief period, media coverage of the war in El Salvador, which had been grotesque, substantially improved. The Administration was compelled to resort to more indirect measures of international terrorism, with consequences that I have already described.

These and many other examples illustrate what can be done under the existing conditions of democracy in the United States. The limits of state coercion leave considerable opportunity for education, organization, and action outside of the formal institutional structures. Those who engage in such efforts will not be sent to concentration camps or psychiatric prisons, and will not be targeted for extinction by death squads. They will, of course, be marginalized or vilified, or simply ignored if the effects of what they do are slight. The efforts can often be frustrating. As late as 1966, for example, it was impossible to hold large public anti-war demonstrations in Boston—perhaps the most liberal city in the U.S.—without concern that they would be violently disrupted—even in churches. Opponents of the war often found themselves speaking to a group of (generally hostile) neighbors gathered in someone's living room, or to audiences in churches or universities of a dozen people, most of them organizers of the event. Widespread efforts of this sort ultimately had an effect, and the movement against the war reached very substantial proportions among the population at large and included very courageous and principled actions of resistance, mainly by the young. The standard version of what happened during those years is in large measure false or even absurd, a reflection of the fears aroused among privileged elites by popular activism that was escaping the control of its "natural leaders." The effects of protest and resistance were not enough to prevent vast massacre and destruction in Indochina. But at least the countries survive in some fashion, more than could have been expected had the protest movement not reached such a scale.

Short of significant institutional change, this is the form that popular efforts to influence state policy will have to take. The ideological system will be careful to exclude serious inquiry or critical commentary on international affairs and security issues. Activism will continue to be largely spontaneous and unorganized, lacking continuity, with little transfer of experience from one episode to the next. This is a consequence of the absence of an opposition press or political parties that are based in such constituencies as labor and the poor, or organizations such as unions that provide a stable and continuing basis for education and social and political action.

Nevertheless, for much of the population, the ideology is paper thin and people can be reached by committed efforts. They can act in many ways to influence the media at least marginally, and to modify decisions reached within the political system from which they are largely excluded. The effects can be quite considerable, very meaningful for the victims of state violence.

The institutions, furthermore, are not fixed for all time. History is not at an end, though it may soon be if significant institutional change does not come about, for reasons I discussed yesterday. The future is open, unpredictable, offering many severe threats and many hopeful possibilities.

Lecture 5: Discussion March 7, 1986

QUESTION: I would like to ask a simple question about ideological coercion. During the invasion of Grenada we know that the U.S. Government stopped journalists from visiting the site for five days. This amounts to press censorship. I'd like to know in what circumstances press censorship has been used in the U.S. over the last 30 years.

ANSWER: Let me begin by pointing out that the American press did protest against that. You remember a couple of times in the discussion I have mentioned several principles of analysis. One of them is that if anything is freely discussed, it is probably unimportant. There are good reasons for that, which I have been trying to explain throughout. Now, in fact, the state did try to impose censorship during the invasion of Grenada, but that was a very insignificant fact. Far more important was the censorship that the press exercised on its own.

Five days before the invasion, the Cuban government had approached the U.S. with an offer of cooperation in taking out the U.S. students. Cuba stated that the Cuban forces, which were very small, would not resist a U.S. landing and would not fire unless they were fired upon by the U.S. forces. After the U.S. did invade, it attacked the Cuban forces who then returned fire. The U.S. government privately recognized that this had happened, and, in fact, on the first day of the invasion there was a kind of weak apology from the U.S. to Cuba, privately. All of this information was available to the U.S. press on the first day of the invasion. That information completely undermines the whole official story about the invasion.

So what happened to this information? The *New York Times* never mentioned it. The next major paper, the *Washington Post*, had a very good Central American correspondent at the time— actually a Latin American woman, I believe. She had a story on the invasion, from Washington, I think. At the very end of her article, where the interesting things usually are, after having given the American propaganda story as the truth, she added a paragraph which said that according to Cuban propaganda, Cuba had proposed cooperation, etc. etc. Now, she knew and everyone else in the U .S. press knew that it wasn't Cuban propaganda. Documents had been released making it clear that it wasn't propaganda.

I don't know the reporter in question personally, but my guess is that she put the information that way so it could reach print.

A little later, I think about a week later, when it was all over, the *Boston Globe*, which is, incidentally, one of the best papers in the country, published an article in which the facts were presented accurately. That was written by one of the editors, and, as far as I know, that's the only discussion of the matter in the U.S. At least in the major press—I don't read all the small town newspapers.

That's crucial suppression of facts. It wasn't state censorship. It is far more important than the fact that the government wouldn't allow the foreign correspondents to go ashore with the Rangers.

The press felt that its professional pride was hurt when they were kept off the landing craft, but they could have told much more important news on the basis of the information that they had. For example I personally have limited resources, but I had all these documents shortly after the invasion, and I don 't doubt for a minute that the press had them too—at once in fact. But they chose to serve the State by suppressing the crucial facts and, incidentally, with the exception that I mentioned, this remains true of the retrospective articles, the histories presented on the anniversary, and so on. That's typical in the U.S., that's the way the system of thought control really works.

Now the question referred to a rare case of state censorship, a matter that wasn't very important, and was therefore widely discussed.

QUESTION: European countries have parties based upon workers. The Socialist parties in countries like Spain and Portugal have renounced the interests that they were supposed to defend. They're going along with NATO and allowing things like unemployment to develop, different factions in the same party, the same as in the U.S.

ANSWER: Remember, what I said was that the parties that are lacking in the U.S.—the labor parties, the Socialist parties, the Communist parties, and so on—are mild reformist parties committed to the state capitalist system but nonetheless rooted in the working class and the deprived part of the population and offering them some means of participation in public policy and to some extent representing their interests. The comment simply illustrates that fact. They are mild reformists, they do not pose a really serious problem to the dominant structure of the Society.

Still they are important. Take England, for example, which is a country very similar to the U.S. in many ways. They have a Labour Party and when that party assumes power, it does pretty much what the Conservative Party docs. Nevertheless, the existence of that party provides a certain continuity for protest activities. So any kind of protest in England, whether over disarmament, or intervention, or whatever, is somehow connected to the Labour Party. In fact, the Labour Party provides a certain limited mechanism by which many sectors of the population, including participants in the labor force, workers, can become engaged in this type of activity. So there is a way of reaching people. There's some degree of continuity and there are even possibilities of learning and building and being a little better next time. That's an interesting and important difference between the U.S. and other industrial democracies.

QUESTION: On Tuesday [lecture 2], you said that détente is a way that the Soviet Union has used to share the war. What kind of connection do you see between this and the U.S. idea that what is going on in Central America is Soviet intervention.

ANSWER: It is certainly true that détente is an idea intended by the Soviet Union as a system of joint global management by the two superpowers, in which the Soviet Union will be a junior partner in world management. In this system each power reserves the right to support allies elsewhere. So, for instance, the U.S. expects to have the right to destroy opposition movements within its own domains. And, in fact, the Soviet Union does not attempt to aid, say, the Salvadoreans or Guatemalans who are being killed by the proxy forces of the U.S.

When conflicts take on an international dimension, the story changes. That's, incidentally, why within the U.S. it was North Vietnam and Nicaragua that became major political issues, whereas the U.S. attack against South Vietnam and its organization of state terrorism in El Salvador did not. The USSR did not raise a finger to try to save the people of South Vietnam, just as they don't in El Salvador. In fact, it's lucky that they don't. If they did, we would not be able to talk about the matter because the world would have blown up. But when the inter-state system is involved then they may support a country against an American attack. That's within the scope of the concept of détente as they understand it. Of course, they insist that the U.S. not intervene if they decide to crush some opposition movement in their own domains. And of course the U.S. does not intervene. So the U.S. did not support Hungarian workers when Russian tanks were killing them. But when the inter-state system becomes involved, then, in fact, the U.S. does give a degree of support, sometimes a lot of support.

Bibliographical Notes

Since the text that precedes consists of edited lectures, there are very few specific references. I have therefore added some references below, lecture by lecture, roughly in the relevant order. For all five lectures, many of the quotes and factual references can be found, with sources given, in my *Turning the Tide* (South End, 1985). Others can be found in earlier books of mine, particularly, *Towards a New Cold War* (Pantheon, 1982), *The Political Economy of Human Rights* (two volumes, with Edward S. Herman; South End, 1979), and *For Reasons of State* (Pantheon, 1973).

Lecture 1

Wm. Roger Louis, *Imperialism at Bay* (Oxford, 1978); Michael Schaller, *The American Occupation of Japan* (Oxford, 1985); R. W. Van Alstyne, *The Rising American Empire* (Oxford, 1960); Stephen Shalom, *The United States and the Philippines* (ISHI, 1981); Melvyn Leffler, "The American Conception of National Security and the Beginnings of the Cold War, 1945-8," *American Historical Review*, April 1984; National Security Council, NSC 5432, "U.S. Policy Toward Latin America," Aug. 18, 1954; *Memorandum for the Special Assistant to the President for National Security Affairs*, "Study of U.S. Policy Toward Latin American Military Forces," Secretary of Defense, 11 June 1965; Thomas M. Franck and Edward Weisband, *Word Politics* (Oxford, 1971); Ruth Sivard, *World*

Military and Social Expenditures 1981 (World Priorities, 1981); Paul Quinn-Judge, *Far Eastern Economic Review*, Oct. 11, 1984 (on casualty estimates in Vietnam); Michael Evangelista, "Stalin's Postwar Army Reappraised," *International Security*, Winter 1982/3.

Lecture 2

Richard Welch, *Response to Revolution: The United States and the Cuban Revolution, 1959-1961* (U. of North Carolina Press, 1985; Eisenhower citation); Edward S. Herman, *The Real Terror Network* (South End, 1982); Noam Chomsky, *Pirates and Emperors: International Terrorism in the Real World* (Claremont, 1986); Julia Preston, *Boston Globe*, Feb. 9, 1986; Dianna Melrose, *Nicaragua: The Threat of a Good Example?* (Oxfam, London, 1985); Gabriel Kolko, *Anatomy of a War* (Pantheon, 1985); George M. Kahin, *Intervention* (Knopf, 1986).

Lecture 3

Council on Hemispheric Affairs, *COHA's 1985 Human Rights Report* (Washington, 1986); "Cerezo's balancing act," *Washington Report on the Hemisphere*, COHA, April 16, 1986; "Amnesty International's Current Concerns in El Salvador," AI Index AMR 29/09/85, Amnesty International, London, June 1985; "El Salvador: Recent Allegations of Torture of Political Detainees," AI Index AMR 29/45/85, Amnesty International, London, October 1985; "Despite Government Pledge, Mass Abuses Continue in El Salvador," *Amnesty Action*, Jan./Feb. 1986; *Settling into Routine*, Americas Watch, May 1986; Ambrose Evans-Pritchard, *Spectator*, 10 May 1986; Allan Nairn, "Confessions of a Death Squad Officer," *Progressive* (March 1986); Bruce Cameron and Penn Kemble, *From a Proxy Force to a National Liberation Movement*, ms., Feb. 1986; Donald T. Fox and Michael J. Glennon, *Report to the International Human Rights Law Group and the Washington Office on Latin America*, April 1985; Michael Glennon,

"Terrorism and 'intentional ignorance'," *Christian Science Monitor,* March 20, 1986; Teófilo Cabestrero, *Blood of the Innocent* (Orbis Books, Maryknoll NY, 1985); Council on Hemispheric Affairs, "Misleading the Public," April 3, 1986 (citing DIA "Weekly Intelligence Summary," July 16, 1982); Joshua Cohen and Joel Rogers, *Inequity and Intervention: the Federal Budget and Central America* (South End, 1986); Bradford Burns, review of *Turning the Tide, Los Angeles Times,* June 8, 1986, on U.S. military expenditures in Central America and combined national budgets; Arthur M. Schlesinger, Jr., *A Thousand Days* (Fawcett Crest, 1967, 704-5), citing Kennedy; Bruce Calder, *The Impact of Intervention* (U. of Texas, 1984); Jan Knippers Black, *The Dominican Republic* (Allen & Unwin, 1986); Piero Gleijeses, *The Dominican Crisis* (Johns Hopkins U., 1986); Cole Blasier, *The Hovering Giant* (U. of Pittsburgh, 1976); Samuel P. Huntington, "American Ideals versus American Institutions," *Political Science Quarterly,* Spring 1982 and correspondence, Winter 1982/3; CBS Document #0606T, 18 April 1986, "Haiti"; Serge Gilles, *Le Monde diplomatique,* Feb. 1986; Lester D. Langley, *The Banana Wars* (U. of Kentucky, 1983); David S. Landes, *New Republic,* March 10, 1986; Hewson A . Ryan, "Haiti: Two centuries of well-intentioned US involvement," *Christian Science Monitor,* Feb. 14, 1986; *Critique of 1985 Department of State's Country Reports on Human Rights,* Americas Watch, May 1986; *Haiti: Human Rights Under Hereditary Dictatorship,* Americas Watch, October 1985; Council on Hemispheric Affairs, *News and Analysis,* Feb. 1, 8, 1986; *Haiti: Family Business* (Latin America Bureau, London, 1985); Robert S. Greenberger, *Wall St. Journal ,* Feb. 10, 1986; Philip S. Foner, *The Spanish-Cuban-American War and the Birth of American Imperialism* (2 volumes, Monthly Review, 1972); Richard Weisskoff, *Factories and Food Stamps: the Puerto Rico Model of Development* (Johns Hopkins U., 1986); Archdiocese of Sao Paulo, *Torture in Brazil* (Vintage, 1986); Douglas R . Shane,

Hoofprints on the Forest: Cattle Ranching and the Destruction of Latin America's Tropical Forests (ISHI, 1986); William H. Durham, *Scarcity and Survival in Central America* (Stanford U., 1979); Dr. Thorn Kerstiens and Drs Piet Nelissen, *Report on the Elections in Nicaragua, 4 November 1984*, on behalf of [Dutch] Government Observers; David Felix, "How to Resolve Latin America's Debt Crisis," *Challenge*, Nov./Dec. 1985; Brian Jenkins, *New Modes of Conflict* (Rand Corporation, June 1983); Inter-American Development Bank Report No. DES-13, *Nicaragua*, Jan. 1983, cited in Penrose, *op. cit.*; Jim Morrell, "Nicaragua's War Economy," *International Policy Report*, Nov. 1985; Morrell, "Redlining Nicaragua," *ibid.*, Dec. 1985; Jim Morrell and William Goodfellow, "Contadora: Under the Gun," *International Policy Report*, May 1986; David MacMichael, testimony, International Court of Justice, Sept. 16, 1985, UN A/40/907, S/17639, 19 Nov. 1985, 26; Thomas W. Walker, *Nicaragua* (Westview, 1986), 71; Ralf Dahrendorf, *Die Zeit*, March 21, 1986 *(World Press Review*, May 1986); Reynaldo Rodriguez, *Survey of the Nicaraguan Economy: 1985*, COHA, Washington, April 8, 1986; Chomsky, "U.S. Polity and Society: the Lessons of Nicaragua," in Thomas Walker, ed., *Reagan versus the Sandinistas* (Westview, 1987).

Lecture 4

Barry M. Blechman and Stephen S. Kaplan, *et. al.*, *Force without War* (Brookings Institution, Washington, 1978); Nathan Twining, *Neither Liberty nor Safety* (Holt, Rinehart & Winston, 1966, 244-5); Editorial, *Washington Post* weekly edition, March 31, 1986; Graham T. Allison, *Essence of Decision* (Little Brown, 1971, I, 39); AP, "McNamara: US near war in '67," *Boston Globe*, Sept. 16, 1983; Donald Neff, *Warriors for Jerusalem* (Simon & Schuster, 1984), on threat of war in 1967; Chomsky, *Fateful Triangle* (South End, 1983), on threats of war in Middle East; Ze'ev Schiff, "The Spectre of Civil War in Israel," *Middle East Journal*, Spring 1985, on inevitability of Israel-Syria war; Desmond Ball , "Nuclear War at Sea," *International Security*, Winter 1985/6; Jeffrey Boutwell and F. A. Long, "The SDI and US Security," *Bulletin of the American Academy of Arts and Sciences*, Feb. 1986; Gorbachev's proposals: AP, April 18, 21, 1986, Serge Schmemann, *New York Times*, and AP, March 27, 1986, on Reagan Administration rejection; Cohen and Rogers, *op. cit.*, on arms buildups; Harold Brown, "Report to Congress on the Budget and Defense Programs," Jan. 29, 1980; Eugene V. Rostow, *Commentary*, Feb. 1979; Downer cited by Bernard Nossiter, *Washington Post*, Dec. 8, 1968; Huntington cited by Cohen and Rogers *op. cit.*

Lecture 5

Leonard W. Levy, *Emergence of a Free Press* (Oxford, 1985); Joshua Cohen and Joel Rogers, *On Democracy* (Penguin, 1983); Thomas Ferguson, "Party Realignment and American Industrial Structure," *Research in Political Economy*, 6.1-82, 1983; Vicente Navarro, "The 1984 Election and the New Deal," *Social Policy*, Spring 1985; Thomas Ferguson and Joel Rogers, "The Myth of America's Turn to the Right," *Atlantic Monthly*, May 1986 and *Right Turn* (Hill and Wang, 1986); Edward Countryman, *The American Revolution* (Hill and Wang, 1985); Gabriel Kolko, *Main Currents in American History* (Pantheon, 1984); Alex Carey, "Managing Public Opinion," ms., U. of New South Wales, 1986; Lawrence J. Freedman, *Inventors of the Promised Land* (Knopf, 1975); Henry David Thoreau, *Journal*, 2 March, 1858, cited by John Dolan in *Thoreau Quarterly*, Winter/Spring 1984; Chomsky, "Visions of Righteousness," *Cultural Critique*, Spring 1986; Dahl, cited by Carey, *op. cit.*; Charles Kadushin, *The American Intellectual Elite* (Little Brown, 1974); Chomsky, *Fateful Triangle*.

Also Available from Haymarket Books by Noam Chomsky

After the Cataclysm
The Political Economy of
Human Rights: Vol. II
with Edward S. Herman
$22, ISBN: 9781608463978

Conversations on Palestine
with Ilan Pappé
$11.95, ISBN: 9781608464708

Culture of Terrorism
$23, ISBN: 9781608463985

The Fateful Triangle
The United States, Israel,
and the Palestinians
Foreword by Edward Said
$24, ISBN: 9781608463992

Gaza in Crisis
Reflections on
the US-Israeli War
Against the Palestinians
with Ilan Pappé
$16.95, ISBN: 9781608463312

Hopes and Prospects
$17, ISBN: 9781931859967,
trade paperback
$39.95, ISBN: 9781931859974,
unabridged audiobook

Intervenciones
Foreword by Eduardo Galeano
$16, ISBN: 9781931859592

Masters of Mankind
Essays and Lectures,
1963–2013
Introduction by Marcus
Raskin, $12.95, ISBN:
9781608463633

Pirates and Emperors,
Old and New
International Terrorism in the
Real World
$18, ISBN: 9781608464012

Powers and Prospects
Reflections on Nature and the
Social Order
$18, ISBN: 9781608464241

Propaganda and the Public Mind
with David Barsamian
$18, ISBN: 9781608464029

Rethinking Camelot
JFK, the Vietnam War, and
U.S. Political Culture
$16, ISBN: 9781608464036

Rogue States
The Rule of Force in World
Affairs
$18, ISBN: 9781608464043

Turning the Tide
U.S. Intervention in Central
America and the Strug-
gle for Peace
$19, ISBN: 9781608464050

The Washington Connection
and Third World Fascism
The Political Economy of
Human Rights: Vol. I
with Edward S. Herman
$19, ISBN: 9781608464067

Year 501
The Conquest Continues
$16, ISBN: 9781608464074

About the Author

Noam Chomsky is widely regarded as one of the foremost critics of U.S. foreign policy in the world. He has published numerous ground-breaking books, articles, and essays on global politics, history, and linguistics. Among his recent books are *Masters of Mankind* and *Hopes and Prospects*. This book and its companion volume, *After the Cataclysm*, are part of a collection of twelve new editions from Haymarket Books of Chomsky's classic works.

© Don Usner

CPSIA information can be obtained
at www.ICGtesting.com
Printed in the USA
JSHW040349020622
26404JS00002B/2

9 781608 464005